T0173109

COMPUTE-IT

COMPUTING

FOR KS3

MARK DORLING
AND GEORGE ROUSE
Series Editors

Contributing authors:
David Ames
Ilia Avroutine
Mark Clarkson
Mark Dorling
Pete Marshman
Sean O'Byrne
Jason Pitt
George Rouse
Carl Turland

DYNAMIC
LEARNING

HODDER
EDUCATION
AN HACHETTE UK COMPANY

CAS recommends this product because it meets the aims of supporting the teaching of computer science within computing to Key Stage 3 pupils. This book supports good practice in teaching the computing curriculum which will help develop computational thinking. It describes good pedagogical strategies and offers progression throughout.

CAS is a grass roots organisation, whose energy, creativity, and leadership comes from its members. We are a collaborative partner with the BCS through the BCS Academy of Computing, and have formal support from other industry partners. Membership is open to everyone, and is very broad, including teachers, parents, governors, exam boards, industry, professional societies, and universities. We speak for the discipline of computing at school level (including FE), and not for any particular interest group. The CAS community has been instrumental in the development of the new curriculum and are 100% committed to supporting all teachers as they engage with computing, and in particular computer science. It contributes to the national debates and consultation regarding the curriculum, assessment, specifications and resources for teaching and learning. It has the aim of promoting and supporting excellence in computer science education.

Further teaching resources are available through the CAS community at:
http://community.computingatschool.org.uk

Hachette UK's policy is to use papers that are natural, renewable and recyclable products and made from wood grown in sustainable forests. The logging and manufacturing processes are expected to conform to the environmental regulations of the country of origin.

Although every effort has been made to ensure that website addresses are correct at time of going to press, Hodder Education cannot be held responsible for the content of any website mentioned. It is sometimes possible to find a relocated web page by typing in the address of the home page for a website in the URL window of your browser.

Orders: please contact Bookpoint Ltd, 130 Milton Park, Abingdon, Oxon OX14 4SB. Telephone: (44) 01235 827720. Fax: (44) 01235 400454. Lines are open 9.00–17.00, Monday to Saturday, with a 24-hour message answering service. Visit our website at **www.hoddereducation.co.uk**

© David Ames, Ilia Avroutine, Mark Clarkson, Mark Dorling, Pete Marshman, Sean O'Byrne, Jason Pitt, George Rouse, Carl Turland 2014.

First published in 2014 by

Hodder Education
An Hachette UK Company
338 Euston Road
London NW1 3BH

Impression number   14
Year   2024

All rights reserved. Apart from any use permitted under UK copyright law, no part of this publication may be reproduced or transmitted in any form or by any means, electronic or mechanical, including photocopying and recording, or held within any information storage and retrieval system, without permission in writing from the publisher or under licence from the Copyright Licensing Agency Limited. Further details of such licences (for reprographic reproduction) may be obtained from the Copyright Licensing Agency Limited, Saffron House, 6–10 Kirby Street, London EC1N 8TS.

Cover photo © adimas – Fotolia

Typeset in ITC Veljovic Std by Phoenix Photosetting, Chatham, Kent.

Printed in India

A catalogue record for this title is available from the British Library.

ISBN 978 1 471 801860

Contents

Introduction

Computing drives innovation in the sciences, in engineering, business, entertainment and education. It touches every aspect of our lives from the cars we drive to the movies we watch and the way in which businesses and governments communicate with and hear from us.

An understanding of Computer Science is essential if you want to keep up with changing technology and take advantage of the opportunities it offers in your life – whether it's as a career or a way of problem solving, or as a way of providing you with a greater appreciation of the way things work.

Computing is a relatively modern area of study but its roots go back to ancient times when our ancestors created calculating devices – long before modern-day calculators came into being. As you'll see, Computer Science also has a rich history of innovation and design.

While it is almost impossible to accurately predict what technological developments will happen next, there are underlying Computer Science concepts and principles that lead to future developments. These can be recognised and applied by people who work in computing.

Computational Thinking is one of these processes and it underpins all the learning in this Student's Book. This should provide you with an approach to problem solving that you will be able to use in relation to a wide range of computer-related and non-computer-related situations. By studying Computer Science you will develop valuable skills that will enable you to solve deep, multi-layered problems.

Throughout this Student's Book we have described the processes that led to the development of major ideas and systems. This will give you a much better understanding of how computing has come to be as it is today. We look at the development of computing through time, from ancient calculating devices to modern technology, highlighting how each breakthrough or development has contributed to modern Computer Science. We look at the elements that make much of the technology we all take for granted today actually work, and we look at how you can apply this knowledge and these skills to computing challenges.

Each unit in the Student's Book centres around a challenge and, in order to gain the knowledge and skills you require to complete each challenge, you will come across three different types of activity:

- **Think-IT**: These are thinking and discussion activities to get you thinking about ideas and concepts.
- Plan-IT: These are planning exercises that set the scene for the practical activities.
- **Compute-IT**: These are the practical computing or 'doing' activities that will allow you to apply the skills and knowledge that you have developed within the unit.

We hope that you enjoy the challenges we have set you and your study of computing.

Mark Dorling and George Rouse

Unit 1 Operating systems

Challenge

Create a poster to explain the similarities and differences between common operating systems to help someone decide which is the best one for them.

1.1 What is an operating system and what does it do?

Key Term

Operating system (OS):
The software that manages a computer's basic functions, such as scheduling tasks, executing applications and controlling peripherals.

What is an operating system?

An **operating system (OS)** is software that manages a computer's basic functions, such as scheduling tasks, executing applications and controlling peripherals.

Not all computers have an operating system. The embedded computer in a microwave or washing machine has a specific set of tasks to perform that never change, so it does not need an operating system. However, including an operating system allows changes to be made, which means that desktops, laptops and mobile devices can serve a variety of purposes, can interact with the user in more complex ways than making basic selections with buttons and can be updated to meet new demands.

An operating system is software that:

- manages the computer's resources, acting as a link between the software and the hardware. Most computers have several programs running at once, all of which require access to the Central Processing Unit (CPU), memory and storage and it is the operating system's role to handle all these requirements and make sure that all the programs will run
- provides a platform for the computer's software to run from

- manages the input and output peripherals such as the mouse, the keyboard and the computer display
- provides the user with an interface, such as a Graphical User Interface or a text-based interface like a command line, to enable them to interact with the computer in a way they can understand
- provides file management, creating files and folders and manipulating, storing and retrieving data
- manages computer start up
- provides utilities, which are small programs that are used for the upkeep and maintenance of the computer
- manages a computer's security, allowing a number of individual users to have their own username and password and using the user's account details to control which files and programs they can access after they have logged on
- allows the user to modify the way the system behaves by setting choices or preferences.

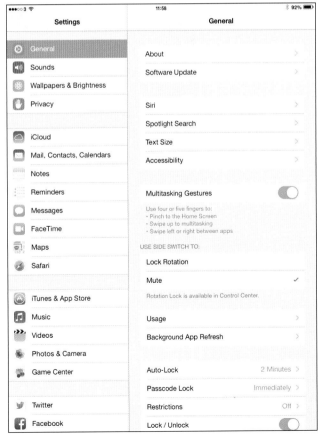

▲ The user interface for changing the preferences on an Apple Mac® computer and an Apple iPad®

Key Term

BIOS: This stands for 'Basic Input/Output System' and the BIOS stores the information required for a computer's boot routine, the routine that runs when a computer is turned on.

Booting the computer

When a computer is switched on it runs some tests on the hardware, checks for new hardware then starts the operating system. This is called the boot routine and we often say we are 'booting up the computer' as a result. The information about the boot routine is stored in the **BIOS** (Basic Input/Output System).

A cold boot is when the user switches on the computer after it has been completely turned off and a warm boot is when the user uses the operating system to restart the computer.

▲ The BIOS chip is part of the motherboard of a computer.

On most computers you can enter the BIOS as the computer boots up. In the BIOS you can change aspects of how the computer boot routine works as well as viewing information about the hardware, for example the temperature of the CPU.

Once the operating system has completed the boot routine, it provides the user with the user interface.

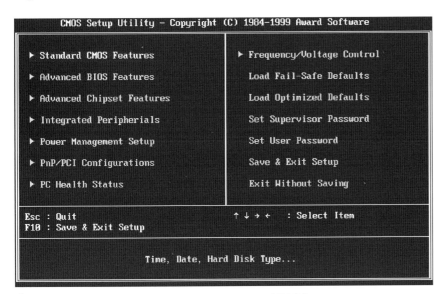

▲ The system settings interface for a typical BIOS

Managing input and output peripherals

A peripheral is a piece of hardware – such as a mouse, a keyboard, a printer or a games controller – that can be attached to and used by a computer and these are managed by the computer's operating system.

If you have ever bought a peripheral device you may have noticed the words 'Plug and Play' on the box. This is because most modern operating systems provide a functionality that automatically detects and configures input and output peripherals without intervention by the user. Not so long ago, when a user plugged in a new peripheral, they would have to install a **driver** to enable the operating system and peripheral to communicate with one another. Now the drivers are automatically installed when the peripheral device is plugged in.

▲ The 'Plug and Play' logo

Key Term

Driver: A driver is software provided by the manufacturer of a peripheral device to enable the operating system and the device to communicate with each other.

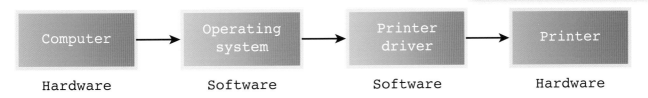

Computer	Operating system	Printer driver	Printer
Hardware	Software	Software	Hardware

▲ Operating systems use drivers to manage peripheral devices.

Managing the computer's resources

Programs and input devices all require CPU time and memory, yet the number of instructions that a CPU can complete per second and the amount of memory available is limited. It is therefore the role of the operating system to manage access to both the CPU and the memory and allocate available resources appropriately to ensure that each application gets a fair chance to make progress.

When you start an application, the operating system loads the necessary parts of the application into memory. It then moves parts of the application into and out of memory as they are required. If parts of the application are not being used then they are removed from memory. Similarly, while you are using an application, some data will be stored in memory but when you close the application this data is removed. This is a very important part of the operating system's role and it is managed by a program called the 'kernel'.

The kernel receives requests to move data into and out of memory from application software and translates these requests into instructions for the Central Processing Unit (CPU) to carry out.

The kernel uses the drivers for each peripheral device and firmware to interact correctly with a device. Firmware is permanent software that is programmed into the read-only memory (ROM) or flash memory of a computer. BIOS is one example of firmware. Firmware is rarely updated after manufacture and in some cases cannot be updated at all.

Think-IT

1.1.1   Sometimes computers appear to slow down. Why do you think this is?

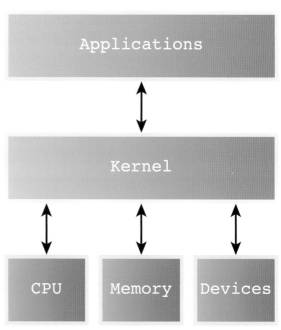

Layers of abstraction

This diagram shows the architecture of a computer as layers of abstraction and it shows the place of the operating system in the architecture.

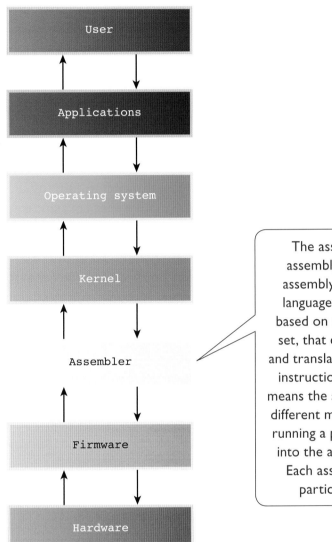

The assembler is programmed using assembly language. You learned about assembly languages in Year 7. Assembly languages are easy-to-remember codes based on the machine's binary instruction set, that can be entered into a computer and translated into the appropriate machine instruction for the CPU to execute. This means the same set of codes can be used on different machines, provided the machine is running a program that translates the code into the appropriate machine instruction. Each assembly language is specific to a particular computer architecture.

These layers of abstraction are a way of hiding the details of each layer. This means that, for example, software developers who are writing applications don't have to concern themselves with the lower layers. They can focus on how the application works with the operating system and can ignore the kernel, the assembler, the firmware and the hardware.

Each operating system has an Application Program Interface (API), which specifies how software applications and hardware such as storage and video cards should interact with each other. This means that if the application meets the requirements of the API it will work in the same way on a range of different computers, regardless of the speed of their CPU and the amount of memory and storage they have, just as long as they all use the same operating system.

The software developer will use a high-level programming language to program the application. High-level programming languages can usually be used with different architectures. However, in order for the operating system belonging to a particular architecture to execute an application, it will need to employ a **translator**. A translator is a utility that translates high-level programming code into machine language that a computer can execute. There are two types of translator:

Key Term

Translator: A translator is a utility that translates high-level programming code into machine language that a computer can execute.

- A compiler is a translator that takes an entire piece of high-level program code and translates it into machine language as a single program before executing it.
- An interpreter is a translator that translates the high-level program code and translates it into machine language one instruction at a time.

Different types of operating system

Desktop or laptop computers and hand-held devices or mobile phones all need an operating system to work, and there are various different operating systems available.

Desktop and laptop computers

For desktop or laptop computers the most common operating systems are:

Windows   Mac OS   Linux

Each of these three operating systems provides a Graphical User Interface with very similar features but some noticeable differences.

Windows® and Mac OS® are proprietary operating systems. This means they are owned by an organisation – Microsoft® owns Windows and Apple owns Mac OS – and can only be modified by that organisation. Linux®, however, is open source. This means that the code for the Linux operating system is freely available for others to modify and there are several versions, or 'distributions', of the Linux operating system available. The most common ones are Ubuntu®, Mint®, Debian® and Fedora®.

Think-IT

1.1.2   Research the Graphical User Interfaces for the Windows, Mac OS and Linux operating systems and identify the similarities and differences between them.

Think-IT

1.1.3   Research the features of the four most common distributions of Linux – Ubuntu, Mint, Debian and Fedora – and write down what you think the strengths and weaknesses of each are.

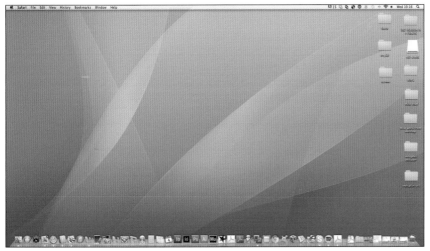

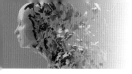

Hand-held devices and mobile phones

Hand-held devices, such as tablet computers, and mobile phones are different to desktop computers and laptops and require different operating systems. Operating systems have been specifically designed to run on these devices and the three most common are Windows Phone®, Apple iOS® and Android™.

▲ The user interface for the Windows Phone operating system

▲ The user interface for Apple's iOS

▲ The user interface for Google's Android operating system

These operating systems do not contain all the features of an operating system designed for a desktop computer or laptop but do perform the same role, linking the user to the software and hardware. They have quite sophisticated Human Computer Interactions (HCI) and allow the user to run various applications, including watching movies, listening to music, managing calendars, playing games and accessing the internet.

Think-IT

I.I.4   Research the HCIs for the three most common mobile operating systems – Windows Phone, Apple iOS and Android – and compare their features. Note down the common features and the differences between them.

1.2 Comparing operating systems

Challenge

Do you remember the challenge for this unit, to create a poster to explain the similarities and differences between common operating systems to help someone decide which is the best one for them? Well, it is time to meet the person you're preparing the information for.

This is Gloria. She is 72 and wants to buy a laptop or a tablet so she can keep in touch with her daughter and granddaughter who have just moved to New Zealand. She does not know much about computers and needs your advice. Which operating system should she be using?

Plan-IT

1.2.1   What are the similarities and differences between the operating systems Gloria could use? Use the information you have gathered by completing 1.1.1 Think-IT, 1.1.2 Think-IT and 1.1.3 Think-IT and any further research you need to do to gather the information you need to prepare your poster.

Compute-IT

1.2.2   Use the information you gathered to complete 1.2.1 Plan-IT to create your poster. Think carefully about how you are going to present your recommendation visually. Are you going to include a comparison table? Images? Facts?

Unit 2 CMD, the command line

Challenge

Your challenge is to start a new job with GCHQ (Government Communication Headquarters) as a forensic analyst. Your first task will involve showing others how to use computers to manage files and folders, before you move on to more advanced file handling techniques that can be used in digital investigations.

2.1 Manipulating files and folders

Graphical User Interface

One of the most common tasks when using a computer is saving a file. It is important to know where you have saved your file and what it is called so that you can find it again. To do this, most people use a **Graphical User Interface** or **GUI** (pronounced 'gooey'). The first part of this unit looks at how to use a GUI to move, rename and delete files and folders.

Using a GUI to move files and create folders seems very simple and straightforward and it is often one of the first things people learn when they start to use computers, but people often have to figure out how to do it for themselves.

Key Term

Graphical User Interface (GUI): An interface that uses graphics rather than text. A GUI can be WIMP (Windows, Icons, Menus and Pointers) but doesn't have to be.

Think-IT

2.1.1 What tasks do older people find easy and what tasks do older people find difficult when they first start using computers?

Naming and organising folders

A new computer user with only three or four files might be okay to just save their files all in the same place. However, once users start building up lots of files, it can become very messy to have everything in one big long list. Using folders to organise files is the best way to keep things tidy and to make it easy to find work again when you need it.

Once users have started to create folders to store their work they will need to give them sensible names. Names that are meaningful make it clear what the folder is about and make it much easier to find work and to make sure files are being saved in the right place. The easiest way to rename a file or folder is to click on it, wait, then click on it again, although you need to be careful you don't double click on the file name and open the file.

▲ 'Silver surfer' is the name given to an elderly person who is a regular or enthusiastic user of the internet. Silver surfers will have had to learn how to use computers much later in life than you.

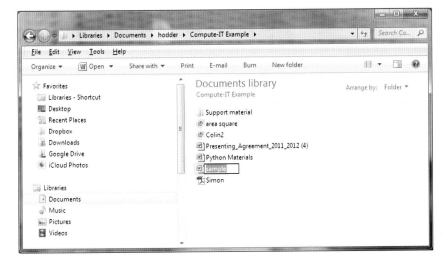

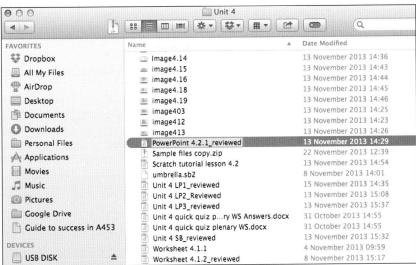

▲ Renaming a file in Windows 7 and in Mac OSX

Drag and drop or cut and paste?

Once a folder structure has been set up, the next step is to move files to the right place. There are two ways to do this.

Users can drag and drop files from their current location into another folder. If the start and end locations are several folders apart, it can be quicker to open two windows and drag the file from one folder in one window to the other folder in the other window.

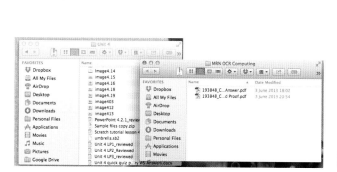

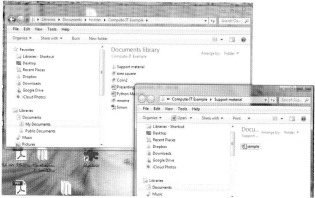

▲ Opening two windows can make it quicker and easier to drag and drop files from one folder to another.

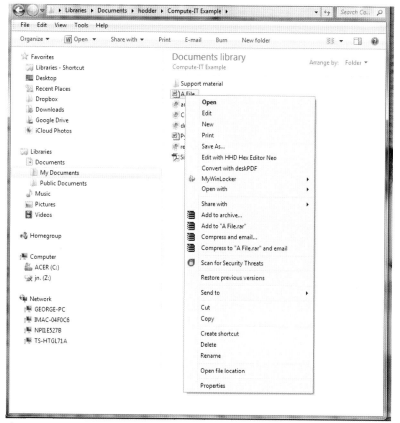

▲ A right mouse click brings up a menu from where you can cut and then paste a file.

Another way to move files is to use cut and paste. You can cut the original file from its original location, just like cutting a picture out of a newspaper, and paste it into its new location.

In Windows 7 there are two different methods to cut and paste a file. You can cut and paste using shortcut keys **ctrl** plus **x** to cut and **ctrl** plus **v** to paste, or you can do it using right mouse clicks.

In Mac OSX you can also cut and paste using shortcut keys but they are slightly different: **cmd** plus **x** to cut and **cmd** plus **v** to paste.

Plan-IT

2.1.2   Develop some materials to advise new computer users on how to manage files and folders correctly.

a)   First, copy and complete the table below:

Task	Why	How
(List the management tasks all computer users should be able to do.)	(Explain why it is important to know how to do each task.)	(Describe how to carry out each task. Where there is more than one method available, describe the one that you consider to be best.)

b)   Then, create a poster, slideshow, word-processed document, screencast or video to advise new computer users on how to improve their file handling habits.

> What criteria are you using to measure 'best'? Is the best method the quickest, the easiest to remember or the easiest to work out how to do if you get stuck?

File extensions

Computer files have two parts to their name, the name and a file extension. For example, a file might be called **Letter to bank.docx**. The name is **Letter to bank** and the file extension is **docx**. The name tells us what the file is about. The extension tells us what kind of file it is and gives us a good clue as to which program to use to open the file.

Think-IT

2.1.3   Match up the file extensions below with the type of file described.

.docx	.mov	.jpg	.exe	.pptx
.html	.bat	.xlsx	.mp3	.pdf

- This is an image file, It could be a photo or a drawing.
- This is a web page and you would normally open it with a web browser.
- This is a popular type of video file.
- This is a document, but usually one that you can't edit.
- This is a file for storing music. You probably have lots of files of this type.
- This is a program and when you double click it the program will load.
- This is a document that you can edit. You would open it with word-processor software.
- This is a spreadsheet document. You would open it with spreadsheet software.
- This is a slideshow. You would open this with presentation software.
- This is a 'batch' file and includes a set of instructions that will run if you double click on it. You might not have seen this type of file much before.

Key Term

Command line: A simple, text-based user interface where commands are typed.

2.2 The command line

While most people use a GUI to move files and folders around there are several reasons to use a **command line** to carry out this kind of task. Computer experts, hackers and forensic analysts often prefer to use a command line. A command line is a simple, text-based user interface where commands are typed.

The first step in using a command line is to open a command prompt. There are different ways to do this depending on the system you are using.

▲ A command prompt in Windows 7. To open a command prompt in Windows 7, Vista and XP, click on the 'Start' menu, then 'All Programs', 'Accessories' and 'Command Prompt'.

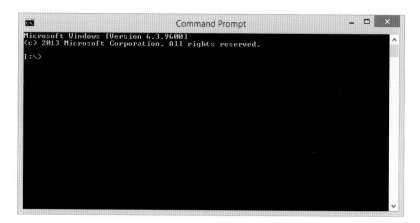

▲ A command prompt in Windows 8. To open a command prompt in Windows 8, swipe in from the right edge of the screen or move the mouse towards one of the right-hand corners and click or tap 'Search'. Then type in 'command prompt'.

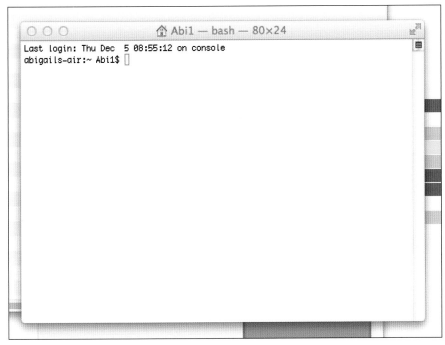

Last login: Thu Dec 5 08:55:12 on console
abigails-air:~ Abi1$ ▯

▲ A command prompt in Mac OSX. To open a command prompt in Mac OSX, open a 'Finder Window', click on 'Applications', 'Utilities' and then 'Terminal'.

By typing commands at the command line it is possible to carry out exactly the same tasks you carry out using a GUI. When using the command line, a folder is normally called a **directory**. For example, the command **mkdir** means 'make a directory' or, in other words, 'create a folder'. Be aware, however, that the commands used at the command line differ depending on your operating system.

Key Term

Directory: A technical name for a folder. The plural is directories.

Compute-IT

2.2.1   Open a command prompt. If your computer system won't let you open a command prompt you could try installing a program such as Console (**sourceforge.net/projects/console**).

Try the following simple commands:

Windows command	Mac / Linux command	Description
cd	pwd	Shows your current directory or location
dir	ls	Lists all the files in that directory
ipconfig	ifconfig	Shows your network configuration

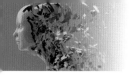

Compute-IT

2.2.2 Open a web browser and go to **www.hoddereducation. co.uk/compute-it**. Download and open Year 8 2.2.2 Compute-IT readme.pdf and follow the instructions.

Whenever you copy, move, delete or rename a file using a GUI, commands like these run in the background. It is actually the commands that copy, move, delete or rename the file, but the GUI acts as an intermediary to make the task easier for the user.

Think-IT

2.2.3 What advantages and disadvantages can you think of for managing files and folders using the command line?

These are the main commands for managing files and folders if you are using a Windows operating system:

Task	Command	Example
Go into a folder or directory	cd	cd myFolder
Go back into the last directory	cd	cd ..
List the contents of a directory	dir	dir
Display the contents of a text file	type	type file.txt
Move a file into a directory	move	move file.txt NewFolder
Copy a file	copy	copy file.txt copy_of_file.txt
Rename a file or directory	ren	ren file.txt new_file.txt
Delete a file	del	del new_file.txt
Make a directory	md	md CMDwork
Delete an empty directory	rd	rd CMDwork

These are the main commands for managing files and folders if you are using a Linux or Mac operating system:

Task	Command	Example
Go into a folder or directory	cd	cd myFolder
Go back into the last directory	cd	cd ..
List the contents of a directory	ls	ls
Display the contents of a text file	cat	cat file.txt
Move a file into a directory	mv	mv file.txt NewFolder
Copy a file	cp	cp file.txt copy_of_file.txt
Rename a file or directory	mv	mv file.txt new_file.txt
Delete a file	rm	rm new_file.txt
Make a directory	mkdir	mkdir CMDwork
Delete an empty directory	rmdir	rmdir CMDwork

2.3 Scripting

Batch files and shell scripts

If you want to run the same three commands several times, for example, one to select some files, one to move them and one to rename them, it is time consuming to type them out each time. Instead, we can create a script or **batch file** or **shell script** that will automatically run all three commands by just running one command.

Batch files and shell scripts are useful for carrying out routine file management on a system. For example, operating systems and applications use log files to record useful information about usage of the system, such as when a user logs on or the addresses of websites that have been visited. These log files can get very large. Imagine how many websites the staff and students in a school visit each year. Batch files and shell scripts are used periodically to rename, move and save log files. In this way, active log files can be kept small and old log files can be archived for access in case of problems or to investigate misuse or attacks.

Creating batch files and shell scripts

If you are using a Windows operating system, the easiest way to create or edit a batch file is by using Notepad. You can also edit a batch file at the command line, although this is a bit more complicated. To make sure the computer knows it is a batch file, simply make sure you save it with a .bat file extension.

If you are using a Mac or a Linux-based operating system then use a plain text editor such as TextEdit or TextWrangler and save your file with a .sh file extension.

Key Terms

Batch file: A simple file in a Windows operating system that contains one or more commands.

Shell script: A simple file in a Mac or Linux-based operating system that contains one or more commands.

Compute-IT

2.3.1 Open a web browser and go to **www.hoddereducation. co.uk/compute-it**. Download and open Year 8 2.3.1 Compute-IT readme.pdf and follow the instructions.

Think-IT

2.3.2 What are the advantages of using a batch file or shell script to repeat a set of commands? What disadvantages can you think of? Can you think of any ways to make batch files and shell scripts even more useful?

Key Term

Wildcard: A symbol that means 'anything', so '*.txt' means 'anything that ends in .txt'.

Using wildcards

The next step on your way to becoming a fully fledged digital investigator is to look at creating more advanced batch files and shell scripts.

Rather than having to type out instructions for each file individually it would be quicker and easier to find all the files ending in '.txt' or all the files with the word 'secret' in their filename and write one command that works on them all at the same time.

The easiest way to do this in Windows is using the following line of code:

```
move *.txt textFiles
```

Using a Mac or Linux operating system you should use the following line of code:

```
mv *.txt textFiles
```

In English, this code reads: move any files that end in '.txt' to the 'textFiles' directory.

Using * as a **wildcard** allows you to do this because it helps you create more complex rules.

You can use multiple wildcards. 'move *secret* secretFiles' would move all the files that have names which start with anything, contain the word 'secret' and end with anything, to the 'secretFiles' folder.

Compute-IT

2.3.3 Open a web browser and go to **www.hoddereducation. co.uk/compute-it**. Download and open Year 8 2.3.3 Compute-IT readme.pdf and follow the instructions.

Challenge

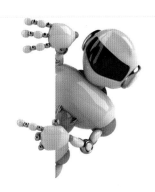

Do you remember the challenge at the start of this unit? You have already started your new job with GCHQ as a forensic analyst and have completed your basic training. It is now time for you to carry out an investigation.

Compute-IT

2.3.4 GCHQ are investigating a series of servers that have been attacked by the notorious hacker HEX. They all contain a similar set of files that the hacker has left behind. We have retrieved the files from the latest server to be hit and zipped them into a file called Year 8 Hex Hacker Files.zip, which you can download from here: **www. hoddereducation.co.uk/compute-it**.

We need you to sort out the files. If you can do this with batch files or shell scripts then we can reuse your work in the future.

a) Create three directories: 'logFiles', 'dataFiles' and 'hackedFiles'.

b) Move any files that end with '.txt' into the 'logFiles' directory.

c) Move any files that have the word 'hex' in the title into the 'hackedFiles' directory.

d) Move the rest of the files into the 'dataFiles' directory.

e) Using a GUI, open all the files in the 'hackedFiles' directory in a text editor. Can you find a hidden message?

f) Using a GUI, open all the files in the 'dataFiles' directory in a text editor. Can you find a hidden message?

▲ The GCHQ building in Cheltenham.

Unit 3 | Binary

Challenge

Create a video tutorial to help students of a similar age learn binary.

Think-IT

3.1.1 **a)** What is the binary string for a woodlouse?

b) What is the binary string for a slug?

3.1 Storing data in binary strings

Binary strings: a brief reminder

Data in a computer is stored in binary. Using binary strings, we can represent pretty much anything we want using just 1s and 0s. The invertebrate key is an example of this. Binary is used to identify an animal, with 01 (no, yes) representing a worm.

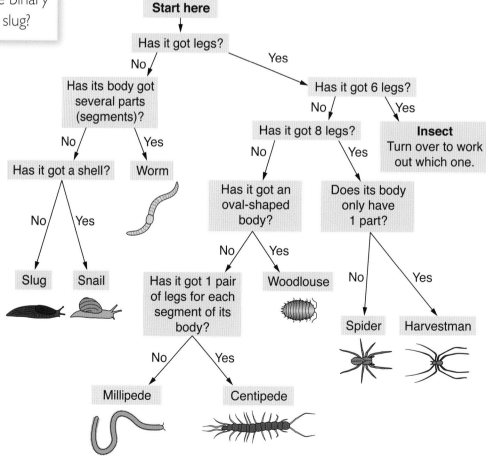

▲ An invertebrate identification key

Counting in decimal and binary

Whole numbers, which are also known as **integers**, can be represented using many different systems, and the term 'base' is used to describe how many different single numbers each different system uses.

'Bi' means '2' in Latin and **binary** only has two numbers available to it (0 and 1), so is known as base 2. 'Deci' means '10' in Latin and the **decimal** number system, which we all use regularly, is known as base 10 because it uses 10 numbers: 0, 1, 2, 3, 4, 5, 6, 7, 8 and 9.

Let's look at an example of a decimal number: 1,536.

> ### Key Terms
>
> **Integer**: A whole number; a number which is not a fraction.
>
> **Binary**: A number system that uses a base of 2 (the numbers 1 and 0).
>
> **Decimal**: A number system that uses a base of 10 (the numbers 0–9).

> When we have counted 10 groups of 10s, we have one group of 100 to add to the 100s column.
> If we count 536 1s we will have the number 5 in the 100s column, the number 3 in the 10s column and the number 6 in the 1s column.

> We start in the first column, which contains 1s. We count from 0 to 9, from the lowest number in the decimal system to the highest. When we reach 9 we have one group of 10 to add to the 10s column. If we continue counting we begin at 0 and count through to 9 again.
> If we count 36 1s we will have the number 3 in the 10s column and the number 6 in the 1s column.

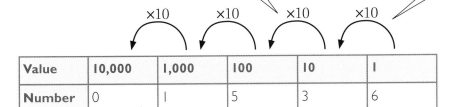

Value	10,000	1,000	100	10	1
Number	0	1	5	3	6

We have:

10^0	1s	1×6	=	6+
10^1	10s	3×10	=	30+
10^2	100s	5×100	=	500+
10^3	1,000s	1×1,000	=	1,000+
10^4	1,0000s	0×10,000	=	0

Total   =   1,536

Think-IT

3.1.2   If decimal is called base 10 and binary base 2 because of the number of numbers they use, what do you think the hexadecimal number system, which is base 16, uses after the number 9? Once you have thought of a number of possibilities, find the answer on the internet.

▼ Binary: The language of computers

Counting in binary

Counting in binary, which is base 2, works in exactly the same way as decimal does except that it only uses two numbers, 0 and 1, instead of 10 numbers, 0 to 9. Each digit in decimal increases by a value of 10, but in binary it increases by a value of 2.

Let's look at an example of a binary number: 10110.

| | ×2 | ×2 | ×2 | ×2 |

Value	16	8	4	2	1
Amount	1	0	1	1	0

We have:

2^0	1s	0×1	=	0+
2^1	2s	1×2	=	2+
2^2	4s	1×4	=	4+
2^3	8s	0×8	=	0+
2^4	16s	1×16	=	16

| Total | | | = | 22 |

So the binary number 10110 is the same as the number 22 in decimal.

Think-IT

3.1.3   Calculate the following binary numbers in decimal.

a) 10   **d)** 11011

b) 111   **e)** 11111

c) 10001

Think-IT

3.1.4   Convert these 4-bit binary numbers into decimal.

a) 1011

b) 1010

c) 1110

Converting binary to decimal

To convert a binary number into a decimal number is nice and easy.

Write the binary bit values on top of or underneath the decimal number and then add up all of those which have a 1 underneath them.

For example, this is how we convert the binary number 110011 to decimal:

1	1	0	0	1	1
32	16	8	4	2	1

32 + 16 + 2 + 1 = 51

110011 in binary = 51 in decimal

Think-IT

3.1.5   Convert these 8-bit binary numbers into decimal.

a) 11010010

b) 01011111

c) 01001101

Converting decimal to binary

To convert a decimal number into binary is relatively simple. There are two main methods.

Method 1

Divide the decimal number by 2. If it divides equally, write a 0. If it doesn't divide equally, and there is a remainder, write a 1.

Divide the result by 2. If it divides equally, write a 0. If it doesn't divide equally, and there is a remainder, write a 1.

Continue until the result is 0.

Write the resulting binary string from right to left, from the smallest to the largest.

For example, this is how we convert the decimal number 13 to binary using Method 1.

13	÷	2	=	6	remainder	**1**					
6	÷	2	=	3	remainder	**0**					
3	÷	2	=	1	remainder	**1**					
1	÷	2	=	0	remainder	**1**	1	1	0	1

13 in decimal = **1101** in binary

Method 2

Find the largest possible binary bit value that can be subtracted from the decimal value without producing a negative number. Write a 1.

Subtract the next largest possible binary bit value from the decimal value. If you can do this without producing a negative number, write a 1. If you do produce a negative number, write a 0.

Write the resulting binary string from left to right, from the largest to the smallest.

For example, this is how we convert the decimal number 13 to binary using Method 2.

13 – 16 = –3 (not possible, so we move on to the next largest bit)

13 – 8 = 5 (we have found our first binary bit)	**1**
5 – 4 = 1	**1**
1 – 2 = –1 (not possible)	**0**
1 – 1 = 0	**1**

13 in decimal = **1101** in binary

Think-IT

3.1.6   Convert these decimal numbers into binary.

  a) 7

  b) 9

  c) 4

Think-IT

3.1.7   Convert these decimal numbers into binary.

  a) 56

  b) 201

  c) 195

Bits, nibbles and bytes

Each unit of binary is called a 'bit'. The term is derived from **B**inary dig**IT**. So 1 bit in binary can represent two numbers, 0 or 1.

Key Term

Bit: Each unit of binary is called a bit. The term is derived from **B**inary dig**IT**. 1 bit in binary can represent two numbers, 0 or 1.

Think-IT

3.1.8 How many numbers can be represented with:

a) 2 bits   **d)** 8 bits?

b) 3 bits

c) 4 bits

Think-IT

3.1.9 Look at your answers to 3.1.8 Think-IT. Can you spot a pattern emerging between the value of the binary units and the number of numbers they represent?

Collections of binary units have different names in computing. As you know, one unit is called a bit, but that is not where the naming stops:

	Name	Example binary
1 unit	A bit	0
4 bits	A nibble	1001
8 bits	A byte	10011101

Key Term

Byte: A string of eight bits, for example, 10010101, is known as a byte.

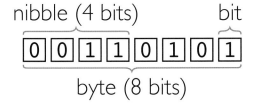

nibble (4 bits)   bit

byte (8 bits)

 A bit, a nibble and a byte

Think-IT

3.1.10 Why do you think 4 bits are called a 'nibble'?

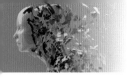

3.2   Binary addition

Binary addition: I + I = IO

Two binary numbers can be added together in a similar way to adding together two decimal numbers. In decimal, if we add two numbers together in a column and the total is greater than 9, we have to carry. The same applies to binary when the total in a column is greater than 1.

Binary sums are not difficult, but it is easy to make a mistake because we are so used to adding using decimal numbers. However, there are only four things we need to remember in binary.

Digit I		Digit 2		Digit 3		Binary	Decimal equivalent
0	+	0	+	0	=	00	0
0	+	0	+	I	=	0I	I
0	+	I	+	I	=	I0	2
I	+	I	+	I	=	II	3

It can be useful to write these combinations down first when adding in binary, so you can refer to them when necessary.

Let's look at this binary sum: 110 + 111.

Stage 1

$$1 \quad 1 \quad 0 \ +$$
$$1 \quad 1 \quad 1$$

Just like in decimal we deal with the column on the furthest right first.

$$0 + 1 = 1$$
$$1 \quad 1 \quad 0 \ +$$
$$1 \quad 1 \quad 1$$

$$1$$

Stage 2

Now we add the second column.

$$1 + 1 = 10$$

1 + 1 in binary equals 10 so we write a 0 and carry the 1 to the next column.

$$1 \quad 1 \quad 0 \ +$$
$$1 \quad 1 \quad 1$$

$$\quad 0 \quad 1$$
$$1$$

Stage 3

Now we add the third column.

$$1 + 1 + 1 = 11$$
$$1 \quad 1 \quad 0 \ +$$
$$1 \quad 1 \quad 1$$

$$\overline{1 \quad 1 \quad 0 \quad 1}$$
$$1$$

Our final answer is 1101.

Think-IT

3.2.I Complete the following binary additions:
- **a)** I0 + III
- **b)** II0I + I0II
- **c)** I00II + I0I
- **d)** III00 + I000I
- **e)** I00II0 + II000I
- **f)** I00I0II + IIII0II

Fixed-length bit string

When we store data we usually store it in a fixed-length bit string of 8 bits.

Binary data stored on your computer is sectioned into blocks and each block is made up of eight connected memory spaces – a byte.

The diagram below shows eight blocks of memory, each block containing one byte. The highlighted block contains the binary number 101 but, as the block contains one byte of space and the remaining bits cannot be left empty, we have to fill them with 0s. This means 101 is stored as 00000101. This is known as a fixed-length bit string. It has to be 8 bits in length and you will often see computational binary represented in 8 bits because of this.

0	1	1	1	0	0	0	1
0	1	1	1	0	0	1	1
1	1	1	0	0	1	1	1
1	1	0	0	0	1	1	1
0	0	0	0	0	1	0	1	←— 101
1	0	1	0	0	0	1	1
0	1	0	0	0	0	0	1
0	0	0	0	1	0	1	0

▲ RAM: The main memory in a computer

Think-IT

3.2.2 Find out how much RAM memory the legendary computer the Commodore 64 had. Why do you think it was this slightly strange number? Why did they not round up to the nearest 10 for example?

Binary overflow

The fact that memory blocks are made up of only 8 bits can lead to problems when dealing with large numbers.

Look at the following sum (255 + 1 in decimal):

> **11111111** +
> **00000001**
> _____
> **100000000**

Can you spot the problem? The answer is 100000000 (256 in decimal), which is 9 bits long. Yet memory blocks are only 8 bits in size and storing just the first 8 bits means the answer is stored in the computer as 00000000 (or 0 in decimal). We therefore have to add a ninth bit. This is called **overflow** and should be noted. There are a number of ways in which computers can deal with the problem of overflow, but we won't be exploring them here. At this point you just need to be aware that overflow is a possibility.

Key Term

Overflow: Overflow happens when the result of a calculation is too large to be stored in the available memory.

Think-IT

3.2.3 Complete the following binary additions:

  a) 11010010 + 00010101

  b) 00110110 + 10101011

  c) 01001101 + 11001101

  d) 01010010 + 00001001

  e) 00001111 + 11110000

Think-IT

3.2.4 Which question from 3.2.3 Think-IT contained an overflow?

3.3 | Teaching others to use binary

Challenge

The challenge for this unit is to create a video tutorial to help students of a similar age learn binary.

Think-IT

3.3.1   Choose which aspect of binary you are going to concentrate on teaching in your tutorial. Will it be binary to decimal conversions, decimal to binary conversions or binary addition? And, if you are focusing on binary addition, will you mention binary overflow?

Plan-IT

3.3.2   Plan your video tutorial as a storyboard.

Compute-IT

3.3.3   Using video editing software, create your video tutorial.

Challenge

Your challenge is to program a 3-bit rover robot to explore efficiently a planet far from Earth, avoiding obstacles it meets along its way.

4.1 Finding the best route

Instructions and your environment

Getting to a destination is something that, as humans, we do every day. Sometimes planning a route from source to destination can be done subconsciously. For example, getting from home to school does not require much planning as you are used to the route you take. Would you be able to describe your route to school to a friend who takes a different route to school? Are there specific details that you would need to provide? When you walk by the park do you cut across the green? When we become accustomed to our environment and to our route we are experts; we know lots of small shortcuts that save time. Those extra little **instructions** are stored in the massive storage we carry around with us: our brains.

Key Term

Instruction: In computer science, an instruction is a command to run some code.

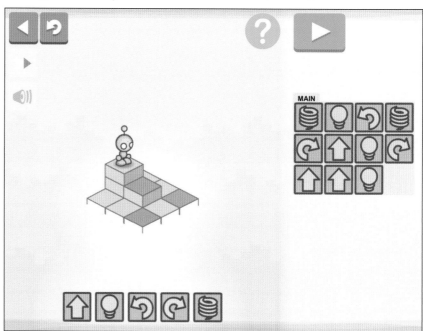

Games such as LightBot are designed to test your ability to get from A to B using as few commands as possible. ▶

Developing a route

Sometimes planning a route from source to destination requires much more planning. Planning a trip to the theatre or to an away football match might involve checking bus and train routes and timetables, as well as finding directions to the venue by foot. Processing all the necessary information can be a fairly simple task using a variety of websites. You might remember all the information, print it out or use a smart device while you are on the move; none of which takes up much storage in your brain and, in the case of using GPS, only requires a small amount of short-term memory. However, you are probably only using common routes and main streets to get to the venue. Because you are not an expert on the journey, you keep the number of different instructions to a minimum to make it as easy as possible to complete.

Programming a robot

Now imagine trying to program a robot to complete the journey from your home to school. It wouldn't be as simple as describing the journey to a friend. Your commands would need to be precise and accurate. Instructions like, 'walk straight down Station Road until you reach a T-junction and then cross over the road and take an immediate left', would not be good enough. How far down Station Road should I walk? Is the road really straight? What does a T-junction look like? Where exactly do you cross? How do you cross safely? Yet, ensuring your instructions are precise and accurate is not the only challenge. Robots don't have the capacity to store and retrieve information and react to situations like our brains can. In fact, the fewer instructions a robot receives to run some code the better, because a lot of instructions use up all of a robot's memory. Taking a long, simple route, which requires only a few commands, might be better than a shorter route that requires more complicated instructions.

Robots are often used to navigate around environments where they are not experts and neither are the people who control them. For example, the NASA Mars Rover has to sense the world around it in order to explore the planet Mars.

▲ Big Trak, an early example of a programmable toy that literally followed directions.

▲ NASA's Mars Rover explores Mars to collect artefacts.

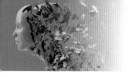
Think-IT

4.1.1   Find out about the Mars Rover and answer the questions.

a) How does the Mars Rover move around Mars?

b) What aspects of the environment on Mars makes it particularly difficult for the Mars Rover to navigate the terrain successfully? What does the robot sense?

c) What inputs does the Mars Rover collect to allow it to navigate the terrain on Mars?

d) What technology is involved to help the Mars Rover navigate the difficult terrain on Mars?

e) Identify three hazards that cause the Mars Rover problems and explain how you could overcome them.

Efficient algorithms

As we know there is usually more than one way to get from A to B. We can analyse the different routes to improve the resulting journey and make it more efficient. But what do we mean by efficient? In what way are we improving the journey?

Efficiency means different things to different people. For example, imagine that you are travelling by car, using a satellite navigation system. Which of the following would you select?

- the fastest route
- the shortest route
- the route that avoids toll roads

> ### Key Term
>
> **Efficiency**: A measure of how much work needs to be carried out to achieve a goal.

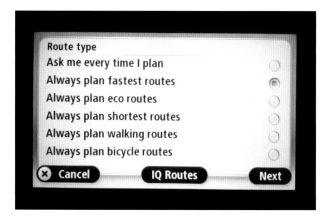

▲ Satellite navigation systems often offer you more than one route. Which will you choose to ensure your journey is efficient?

The fastest route is likely to be time efficient, the shortest route is likely to be fuel efficient and avoiding toll roads is likely to be money efficient. But what happens if you discover that the shortest route involves driving up and down lots of hills and uses more fuel? Or what if avoiding toll roads involves a longer journey that uses more fuel and ends up costing more? Which route is the most efficient now? To answer this question we have to decide in which way we wish to be efficient or which combination of our requirements we are optimising for. Is it fuel, time, or money?

Plan-IT

4.1.2 Create a robot and a planet for your robot to explore.

a) Draw a 12 × 12 grid on a piece of squared paper. Label the rows 0 to 11 and the columns A to L.

b) Draw six obstacles that the robot might encounter on your planet while it is exploring.

c) Draw a small robot on a square of paper the same size as the squares your planet is made up from. Place your robot anywhere on your planet.

d) Mark one square on your planet, some distance away from your robot, with an X. This is your destination.

Plan-IT

4.1.3 Using the planet you made in 4.1.2 Plan-IT, work out two different routes for your robot to take from its starting point to X avoiding the obstacles on the way. Your robot will only respond to the following instructions:

■ Forward: moves one square forwards in the direction the robot is facing
■ TurnLeft : turns to the left 90 degrees
■ TurnRight: turns to the right 90 degrees
■ Backward: moves one square in the opposite direction to the direction the robot is facing.

For each route, record every instruction you give to your robot and, when you have reached your destination, count up how many instructions you used and how many times you used each of the four instructions.

Think-IT

4.1.4 Look at the routes you recorded for 4.1.3 Plan-IT.

a) Which route used the least number of instructions?

b) Which route used the least number of different instructions?

c) Which route do you think is the most efficient?

A robot moving across terrain might be able to get from A to B using the shortest route around the obstacles in its way, but if the route meant it had to turn left and turn right lots of times then the shortest route may not be the fastest route because it requires a lot more commands. Often we have to weigh up the pros and cons of different routes before making a decision about which is more efficient.

More instructions, more bits

As you know, data is stored on a computer in binary, in 1s and 0s. Decimal numbers can be represented by unique binary strings, and so can instructions. For example, an **encoded** two-bit robot could carry out the following instructions, one instruction for each unique combination of the two bits:

00 = **Forward**
01 = **TurnLeft**
10 = **TurnRight**
11 = **Backward**

An **instruction set** is the group of instructions a machine can carry out. A two-bit instruction set will only enable a robot to perform four moves. Having more instructions will allow a robot to do more. For example, with instructions to climb over, to hover over or to dig under, it could avoid obstacles in its path, and it could adapt to night time and day time if it had lights on and lights off instructions.

> ### Key Terms
>
> **Encoded**: When an instruction has been coded as a binary representation it has been encoded.
>
> **Instruction set**: The group of unique instructions a machine can carry out.

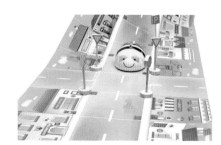

BeeBots can navigate around a map using four instructions, which could be represented as a two-bit instruction set. ▶

Think-IT

4.1.5 Think of your walk to school or, if you don't travel by foot, imagine you are walking the route that you usually take.

a) Is it possible to get to school using just the four basic instructions: Forward, Backward, TurnLeft and TurnRight?

b) If it would not be possible, how many extra instructions – such as OpenGate or CloseGate – would you need to be able to get to school?

c) If you were to take a shortcut to school, how many more instructions – such as SwimAcrossRiver or ClimbSteps – would you need?

d) Create a table, giving a unique binary representation to each of your instructions.

e) Calculate how many bits you would need to encode your instructions.

Plan-IT

4.1.6 a) Using the planet you created for Plan-IT 4.1.2, think of two new instructions – such as MoveStones or HoverOverRavine – to add to your robot's instruction set that would allow it to find a quicker route to its destination.

b) Work out two different routes for your robot to take from its starting point to X, which will make good use of your two new instructions. For each route, record every instruction you give to your robot and, when you have reached your destination, count up how many instructions you used and how many times you used each instruction.

Think-IT

4.1.7 Compare the routes you recorded for your robot when it had a shorter instruction set (4.1.3 Plan-IT) with the routes you recorded for 4.1.6 Plan-IT, where your robot has a larger instruction set.

a) Which instruction set – the smaller or the larger – generated the least number of instructions?

b) Which instruction set – the smaller or the larger – used the least number of different instructions?

c) Which instruction set – the smaller or the larger – do you think produced the most efficient journey?

More instructions mean more bits and more bits mean the robot needs a larger memory to store them all. As the size of the memory increases, the cost of the robot also increases. The robot becomes more time consuming and complicated to program too. However, more instructions means a robot has more functionality and can probably complete a task more efficiently and adapt to different circumstances better as a result.

The importance of a good algorithm

Simply having a larger instruction set does not ensure a robot works more efficiently though. It must also be programmed with an algorithm that makes good use of the instructions available.

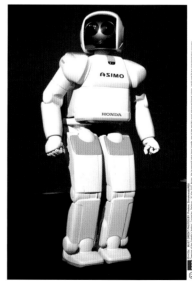

▲ A vacuum cleaning robot has a small instruction set whereas the Honda Asimo robot, a humanoid robot, has a large instruction set.

Think-IT

4.1.8 a) Look at the map and the three algorithms below. First rank the algorithms in order of simplicity and then rank them in order of efficiency. Explain your ranking decisions.

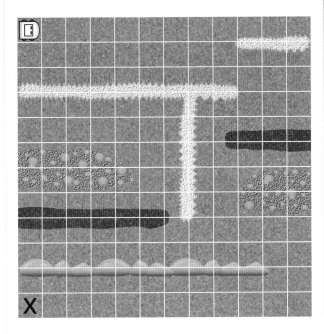

Algorithm 1	Algorithm 2	Algorithm 3	
Right	Forward	East	West
Forward	Forward	East	West
Forward	Forward	East	West
Climb	Forward	East	West
Forward	Forward	East	West
Scoop	Forward	East	West
Forward	Forward	East	West
Scoop	Right	South	West
Forward	Forward	South	West
Saw	Climb	East	West
Forward	Forward	South	
Smash	Forward	West	
	Forward	West	
	Forward	South	
	Forward	South	
	Smash	South	
	Forward	South	
	Right	South	
	Forward	East	
	Forward	East	
	Forward	East	
	Forward	South	
	Forward	South	
	Forward	South	

b) Each instruction used in the three algorithms takes a different length of time to execute.

Instruction	Time to execute (seconds)
Forward	10
Right	10
Left	10
South	20
West	20
East	20
Climb	60
Scoop	30
Saw	120
Smash	60

The total time taken to complete each algorithm is therefore as follows:

- Algorithm 1 = 370 seconds
- Algorithm 2 = 350 seconds
- Algorithm 3 = 340 seconds

Does this change your simplicity ranking? Does this change your efficiency ranking? Why?

4.2 Programming a robot with a 3-bit instruction set

Choosing the best instructions

As you know, programming a robot with a vast range of instructions so it can adapt to almost anything requires a lot of memory, which is expensive. The algorithms required to run the instructions are also very complex. It is therefore important to home in on the right instructions for a particular task and only program your robot with the instructions it needs. To do this, you need to think about the instructions that will be used a lot and those that will make the activity more efficient before you begin programming.

▲ Smartphone app libraries allow us to install instructions for our mobile device, but we choose those that we require and those that we will use most.

Think-IT

4.2.1 a) Robon Jovi has always wanted to be a rock star. Now is her chance. She's been drafted into the world's most famous band following a short circuit to the band's lead guitarist. This could be the big break she has been waiting for, so she wants to put on an awesome performance. Although Robon is a 3-bit robot, she would like to keep her instructions to a minimum to ensure super efficiency but, at the same time, she wants to make an impact on stage.

Which eight of the following instructions should Robon use to form her 3-bit instruction set?

Break Guitar Over Leg	Move Right Hand Up	Move Right Hand Down	Move Left Hand Up
Move Left Hand Down	Tune Guitar	Bow	Break Guitar Over Leg
Sleep	Clap	Strum Strings	Pick String
Place Finger On String E (Thick)	Place Finger On String B	Place Finger On String G	Place Finger On String D
Place Finger On String A	Place Finger On String E (Thin)	Remove Fingers From Strings/Frets	Jump
Left Leg Up	Right Leg Up	Left Leg Down	Right Leg Down
Left Hand Up	Right Hand Up	Left Hand Down	Right Hand Down
Head Up	Head Down	Smash Guitar On Floor	Do Splits
Smile	Throw Plectrum Into Crowd	Throw Guitar Into Crowd	Fall On Knees

b) Next to each instruction you have chosen, write a 3-bit binary representation.

Using a graphical programming language to simulate a robot's instruction set

We can use procedures in a graphical programming language to simulate the instructions in an instruction set, with each procedure corresponding to one instruction in the instruction set. As you discovered in Compute-IT 1, a **procedure** is a section of code that can be used over and over again and which can accept input from other parts of the program. The main program can then call on each procedure when it needs it. When the procedure receives the **call** – the input – from the main part of a program, the instructions within the procedure are executed. When the procedure has been executed, the main part of the program continues to run. The main part of a program can combine and repeat procedures as necessary.

> ## Key Terms
>
> **Procedure**: A procedure is a section of code that can be used over and over again. It can accept input from other parts of the program.
>
> **Call**: When the main part of a program wants to run a procedure it calls it.

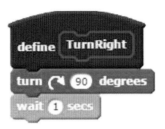

Compute-IT

4.2.2 Using a graphical programming language, create your own planet and rover and, using procedures, program your rover to explore the planet.

a) Create a background using two different colours, one for the terrain the rover has to pass through and one for the route the rover will take to reach its destination.

b) Create your rover as an object or sprite.

c) Code three instructions, such as Forward, TurnLeft, TurnRight, as procedures.

d) Code your main program, which calls on the procedures to enable your rover to reach its destination.

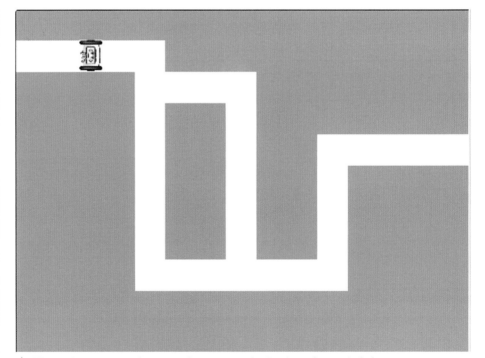

▲ This is how your planet and rover might look in Scratch 2.0.

▲ This is a Scratch 2.0 program. The main part of the program identifies the main route through the code. It calls on the three procedures – Forward, TurnLeft and TurnRight – when it wants to use them.

Controlling a robot with real-time instructions

Up until now the rover has moved according to a set of predetermined instructions because we knew the path it had to take before it began its journey. But what if we couldn't see ahead like this? How do we provide the rover with its instructions in real time?

As you know, each instruction has a unique binary representation. The program can be adapted to accept direct instructions from a user so that the robot responds to these in real time rather than having to devise a scheduled sequence of instructions in advance. By adding blocks that define the binary input as instructions for the robot, it can be controlled by entering the appropriate binary representation. For example 00 = Forward, 01 = TurnLeft and 10 = TurnRight.

Overcoming obstacles

A small instruction set for a robot can be very efficient in terms of the memory needed for instructions, but a small instruction set may not enable the robot to perform the tasks needed. Being able to foresee problems is all part of being a good programmer. Imagine that you sent a rover to Mars and the rover got stuck inside a crater and you hadn't programmed it with the instructions that enable it to climb out of the crater. The rover would not be able to complete its mission, which could be embarrassing and costly.

Compute-IT

4.2.3 Adapt the program you created for 4.2.2 Compute-IT so that your rover moves as you provide new binary commands for it to follow.

- Create a command that asks the user to enter a binary representation.
- Provide three 'if' selection statements that check to see if the answer is 00, 01 or 10.
- Each 'if' statement should then call the right procedure.
- Wrap a 'forever' loop around your 'if' statements so that the program will continue to ask for the next command.
- Run your program and debug the errors that you find within your code.

Think-IT

4.2.4 Imagine your rover was on a planet that could support plant life and possibly even animal life. What five obstacles might it come across and how could it be programmed to overcome them? Copy and complete the table below.

Obstacles the rover might encounter, for example, water and trees	Name of instruction which will deal with the obstacle and the binary representation assigned to the procedure	Description of how you might program your rover so that the image on the screen visually illustrates how it is overcoming the obstacle

4.3 Assessing the efficiency of a 3-bit instruction set

Challenge

◀ The Mars Rover collects data about the terrain on Mars, which is stored on board and then sent back to Earth to help build up a map of the planet's surface. Obstacles and possible routes around them are recorded.

The challenge for this unit is to program a 3-bit rover robot to explore efficiently a planet far from Earth, avoiding any obstacles it meets along the way.

As we know, efficiency is determined by our requirements or what we are trying to optimise. One method of calculating the efficiency of a route is to calculate the total number of bits used. The fewer bits required to complete a route, the more efficient it is. Having more instructions will provide more options for the robot and might make the route quicker, but more instructions means more bits for each instruction, making the bit count for each movement higher. For example, three 2-bit instructions will have the same bit count as two 3-bit instructions. It is therefore necessary to trade off the total number of instructions available against the number of instructions required to complete the route.

Compute-IT

4.3.1   The program you created in 4.2.3 Compute-IT should include at least two different routes for your rover to reach its destination:

a) Add a bit counter to the program you created in 4.2.3 Compute-IT. You are currently using 2-bit instructions so each time a procedure is called, a variable – TotalBits – should increase by two. Ensure that the variable TotalBits resets to 0 when the program is restarted.

b) Run your robot through each of the routes and work out which uses the smallest number of bits.

Compute-IT

4.3.2 a) Add some obstacles blocking the paths you created for 4.3.1 Compute-IT.

b) Create two new procedures to enable your rover to pass the obstacles.

c) Adding two new instructions will increase the number of bits used for all instructions, so edit your program so the bit counter – TotalBits variable – increases by the right number of bits each time an instruction is executed.

d) Building on your work for 4.2.4 Think-IT, program your rover so that the image on the screen visually illustrates how your rover is overcoming the obstacles.

e) Now run your robot through each of the routes and work out which uses the smallest number of bits.

How big are programs that use 3-bit instruction sets?

Throughout this unit, we have been working with 2-bit and 3-bit instruction sets. But how big are the programs that use 2-bit and 3-bit instruction sets? And how many programs that use 2-bit and 3-bit instruction sets would the memory of an average laptop hold?

Back in 1987, the Commodore Amiga 500 was one of the most popular and powerful home PCs available on the market. It came with 512 KB of RAM. A rover with a 3-bit instruction set that is programmed to perform a task that requires 30 instructions will require 90 bits of memory (30 × 3). A 3-bit instruction set is a fixed size. There are 8 bits in a byte, so the Commodore Amiga 500 was able to hold 4,194,304 bits (512 × 1024 × 8). That works out at 46,603 programs of 30 instructions each for instructions taken from a 3-bit instruction set (4,194,304 / 90).

Memory has moved on significantly since the late 1980s. A new computer or laptop can now have 8 GB of RAM, which means it can store 745,654 sets of 3-bit instructions containing 30 instructions.

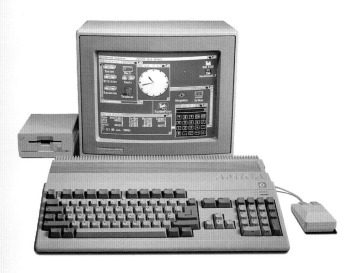

Think-IT

4.3.3 Imagine you are programing a 4-bit robot with 4,000 instructions. The robot has a memory of 1 KB. Could the robot hold all 4,000 instructions?

▲ The Commodore Amiga 500 came with 512 KB of RAM when it was launched in 1987.

Programming using selection statements and Boolean expressions

Challenge

Your challenge is to program a robot that appears to be intelligent – a robot that can successfully navigate around a maze all by itself.

5.1 'If' selection statements and Boolean operators

Key Terms

Selection: The name given to the process of providing possible courses of action that will be selected as a result of certain conditions being met.

Decompose: Breaking a problem down into a series of simpler problems that we can easily understand. The process of decomposing a problem is known as 'decomposition'.

Using selection to make decisions

As you know from Compute-IT 1, humans use **selection** when they decide which course of action they will take in a particular set of circumstances. The most common form of selection is an 'if' statement. For example:

- if it is raining, take a coat
- if it is dry, don't take a coat.

Yet, as you also know from Compute-IT 1, a seemingly simple task like taking a coat – or brushing your teeth – must be **decomposed**. You must identify the actor and the actions and how they work together to complete the required task. Taking a coat could be decomposed like this:

- Go to coat pegs in hallway.
- Identify coat.
- Remove coat from coat peg.
- Put coat on.
- Zip coat up.
- Pull hood up.

Think-IT

5.1.1 Identify a decision you made this morning using 'if' selection. Decompose the task you completed after making the decision.

When programming, it is rare to be able to complete a task without encountering more than one 'if' statement. For example, is there a door between you and the coat pegs in the hallway? Is the door open or closed? As a human, you will use your senses to decide how to act in each situation. However a robot doesn't have human senses. Instead, robots have **sensors** to help them answer the questions raised by the process of selection.

> **Key Term**
>
> **Sensor**: A device that detects or measures the environment around it.

Think-IT

5.1.2 **a)** List the senses you have, as a human.

b) From the list of senses you have as a human, identify those that will help you complete the task of taking a coat with you when you leave home.

Think-IT

5.1.3 What sensors do robots have that enable them to sense the same things that humans sense?

> **Key Term**
>
> **Abstraction**: Working with ideas or solving a problem by identifying common patterns in real situations, concentrating on general ideas and not the detail of the problem itself.

Abstracting a problem before programming

The challenge for this unit is to program a robot that can navigate around a maze all by itself. It's a complex task and, at first glance, it seems almost impossible. But we can use **abstraction** to help us break the task down into something more manageable.

Let's apply abstraction to the maze itself first of all. When you think of a maze, do you think of something like this?

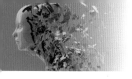

However, if all the variations are stripped away – what the maze is made out of, how big it is and how complicated it is for example – then a maze can be simplified and drawn on a grid so that it looks like this:

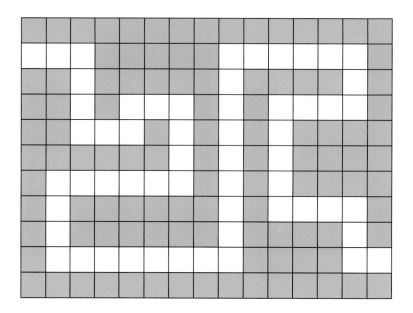

Now let's apply abstraction to the robot. What does a robot absolutely have to do to be able to move around the maze? It needs to be able to move forwards and to turn left and right and it needs three touch (or proximity) sensors to be able to decide which instruction it should execute at any given moment. Because the three sensors are all the same, it is a good idea to give them each a different colour to make them unique. With its sensors, the robot would look as shown on the left:

Programming selection to make decisions

The robot will use input from its sensors to decide how to move. We could consider using the following algorithm:

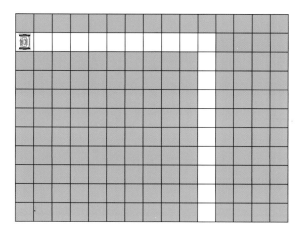

- If pink senses white path, move forward.
- If pink senses green maze wall, turn right 90 degrees.

If the maze looked like this, then this set of instructions would get the robot to the end of the maze.

But what if the maze looked like this?

You would need to add a left turn to your instruction set:

- If pink senses white path, move forward.
- If pink senses green maze wall, turn right 90 degrees.
- If pink senses green maze wall, turn left 90 degrees.

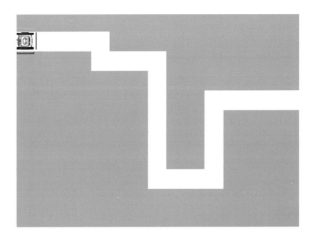

But the robot would not be able to turn left if it was programmed with the above instruction set because the input for both the turn right instruction and the turn left instruction are exactly the same. There is a conflict. For the robot to sense whether it needs to turn right or turn left, we need to create three unique 'if' statements using three sensors:

- If pink senses white path, move forward.
- If blue senses white path, turn right 90 degrees.
- If green senses white path, turn left 90 degrees.

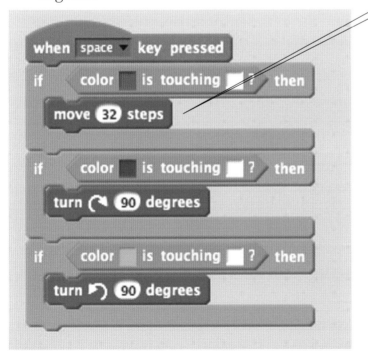

▲ Three unique IF statements programmed in Scratch 2.0

> This is set to 32 because the robot needs to move 32 steps forwards to travel the distance of one square in the maze.

Compute-IT

5.1.4 Using a graphical programming language, create a maze and a robot with three coloured sensors. Then, program your robot to move through the maze – moving forward, left and right – using three 'if' statements.

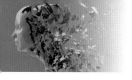

Refining code with AND and OR Boolean operators

We could use the following 'if' statement to decide what to pack for school:

- IF I have physical education, THEN pack all sports kit.

However, if you know that you will only be playing tennis this term, then you will be carrying lots of sports kit that you do not need. We therefore need to refine the 'if' statement and make it more sophisticated. We can do this using the **Boolean operators** AND and OR:

- IF I have physical education AND it is tennis, THEN pack tennis kit.
- IF I have physical education AND it is hockey, THEN pack hockey kit.
- IF I have a tennis match OR it is tennis practice, THEN pack tennis kit.
- IF I have a hockey game OR it is hockey practice, THEN pack hockey kit.

Boolean operators can help us make decisions based on more than one item of information.

Imagine for a moment that the maze is actually a circuit with a finish line. We would need to tell the robot to move forwards when the pink sensor senses the white path 'or' the black line so that the robot crosses the finish line and continues on around the circuit.

Key Term

Boolean operators:
Connective words – AND, OR, NOT – which can be used to construct a more sophisticated condition from which a computer program can make decisions.

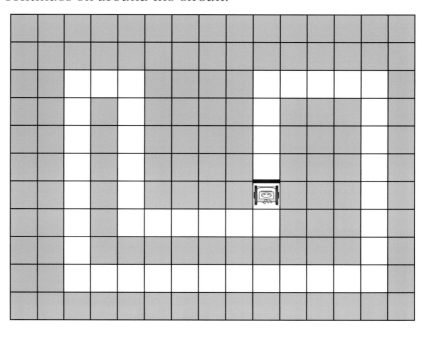

The robot can move forwards if its pink sensor senses white OR black. ▶

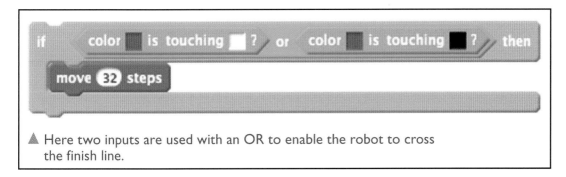

▲ Here two inputs are used with an OR to enable the robot to cross the finish line.

If we wanted to control the number of times the robot completes the circuit we could include a lap counter variable that increases by one every time the robot passes the black finish line.

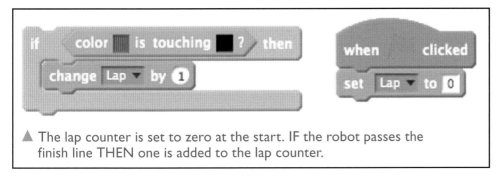

▲ The lap counter is set to zero at the start. IF the robot passes the finish line THEN one is added to the lap counter.

We can now control the number of times the robot passes through the finish line and stop it when it has completed a set number of laps.

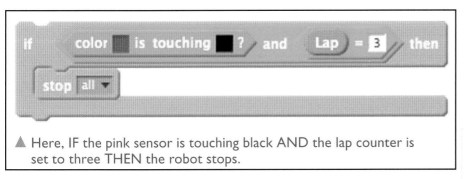

▲ Here, IF the pink sensor is touching black AND the lap counter is set to three THEN the robot stops.

Compute-IT

5.1.6 Using a graphical programming language, create a circuit and a robot with three coloured sensors. Then, program your robot to move around the circuit three times when you hold down a key.

Plan-IT

5.1.5 a) Write an algorithm for a robot so that it moves around a circuit regardless of whether or not the finish line is in front of it.

b) Add to your algorithm so that a lap counter increases by one when the robot passes the finish line.

c) Amend your algorithm so the robot stops when the lap counter reaches three.

5.2 Nesting selection statements and the NOT Boolean operator

Key Term

Nesting: Placing a section of code within another section of code.

Nesting selection statements

A section of code is **nested** when it is placed within another section of code. In this example of code for a web page, which is taken from Compute-IT 1, **<title>Your Awesome Webpage</title>** is nested within the code for the document header.

```
<!doctype html>
<html>
  <head>
    <title>Your Awesome Webpage</title>
  </head>
  <body>
    <p>Make something amazing with the web</p>
  </body>
</html>
```

Selection statements can be nested and nested selection statements can be seen as a sequence of decisions that are taken to refine a large data set into a smaller data set that meets your specific needs. This is an example of decomposition, where a complex problem is broken down into simpler problems.

For example to find men's blue jeans we can search clothing by men's, then jeans then blue.

```
IF 'men's clothing' THEN
  IF 'jeans' THEN
    IF 'blue'
```

Think-IT

5.2.1 What other examples of nesting are there in the section of code above?

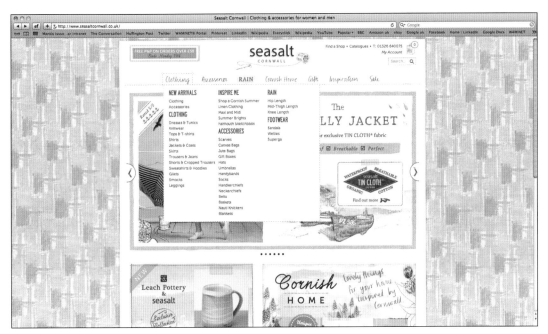

▲ The filters on an online shopping website act like a series of 'if' statements. Each filter is an 'if' statement that is executed on the data output from the previous 'if' statement, refining the results returned to narrow your options.

How do nesting selection statements make a robot appear intelligent?

We know how to program a robot to follow a path using one sensor at a time. By testing two conditions using two sensors, and combining the results, we can provide a better picture of the situation. For example, if it is raining we need to decide whether we are going to take a raincoat or an umbrella, but if we also know that it is windy we will choose the raincoat.

> **If it is raining Then**
>   **If it is windy Then**
>   **Take raincoat**

Using more than one sensor makes a robot appear more intelligent because it can avoid obstacles it comes across rather than just follow a path. This is similar to the algorithms that NASA's Mars rovers use to navigate across the unknown terrain of the red planet.

Plan-IT

5.2.2 Draw a flowchart to illustrate the example provided above.

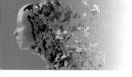

Compute-IT

5.2.3 This Scratch 2.0 program shows how two nested 'if' statements can be used so that an action is performed if both conditions are true. What changes can you make to the code so that the program uses only four 'if' statements rather than five?

```
when space ▾ key pressed
if    color ■ is touching □ ? then
    move 32 steps

if    color ■ is touching ? then
    if    color ■ is touching ? then
        turn ↺ 90 degrees


if    color is touching ? then
    if    color ■ is touching ? then
        turn ↻ 90 degrees
```

Think-IT

5.2.4 Why might it be better to have fewer 'if' statements?

Compute-IT

5.2.5 Adapt the program you created for 5.1.4 Compute-IT so that your robot uses two sensors and nested 'if' statements to navigate through your maze.

Key Term

Venn diagram: A visual way of showing categories of objects that, when they fit two or more conditions, become a new category.

Venn diagrams

Venn diagrams were invented around the year 1880 by John Venn and can be used to illustrate concepts from computer science and a number of other areas.

We can illustrate the use of Boolean operators such as AND and OR using Venn diagrams. Venn diagrams are often drawn inside a rectangular box. The rectangular box represents the search domain or the set of all possible answers.

For example, our shopping search with nested loops can be illustrated using a Venn diagram:

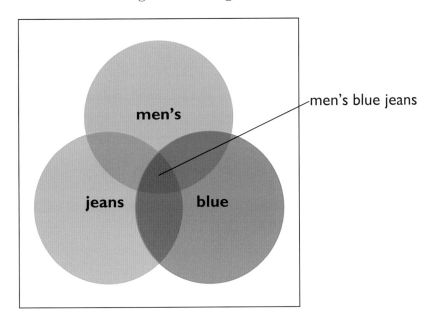

Consider the three laws of robotics by science fiction author Isaac Asimov:

- **First law:** A robot may not injure a human being or, through inaction, allow a human being to come to harm.
- **Second law:** A robot must obey orders given to it by human beings except where such orders would conflict with the First law.
- **Third law:** A robot must protect its own existence as long as such protection does not conflict with the First or Second law.

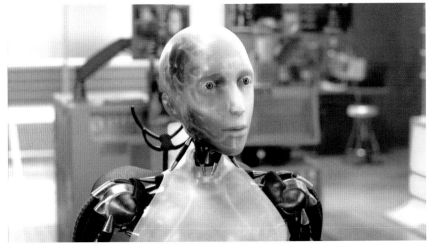

▲ *Sonny* the robot from the film *I Robot* based on Isaac Asimov's three laws.

It would be dangerous enough if a robot failed to follow one of these laws, but imagine if a robot failed all of the laws.

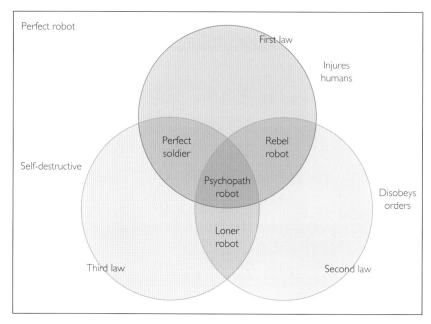

▲ A Venn diagram showing what might happen if robots broke the laws of robotics.

Compute-IT

5.2.6 Write a program that identifies what kind of robot it would be if a robot broke at least one of Isaac Asimov's three laws of robotics. Use the Venn diagram above to help you.

a) Complete the truth table, identifying what combination of true and false relates to each type of robot.

	Obeys First law: does not injure humans	Obeys Second law: obeys orders	Obeys Third law: not self-destructive
Psychopath robot	False	False	False
Robot rebel			
Perfect soldier			
Injures humans			
Loner robot			
Disobeys orders			
Self-destructive			
Perfect robot			

b) Write the pseudocode that shows how your truth table can be turned into a program.

Combining the Boolean NOT operator with 'if' selection statements

When communicating with each other we often reverse the meaning of words using the word 'not'. For example:

- I will not do my homework.
- I cannot do my homework
- I don't do my homework.

Like AND and OR, **NOT** is a Boolean operator. And, when programming, it is often easier to create instructions that remove the wrong actions than list all the correct actions. It certainly makes the code much easier to debug!

Think about our robot in the maze. At the moment, the colour of the land that is not the path through the maze is green. But what if the background was red and green? The instructions are so specific that introducing red into the background would mean the robot wouldn't be able to navigate the path through the maze, because the sensors are only checking for green. However, if we use the NOT Boolean operator, we can reprogram the robot so that its sensors check for land that is NOT white. The background can then be any colour you want it to be; except white.

> **Key Term**
>
> **NOT**: This Boolean operator reverses the input so, for example, if the input is 'true' it will be converted to 'false' and vice versa.

> **Compute-IT**
>
> **5.2.7** Amend the program you created for 5.2.5 Compute-IT so that your robot can navigate the maze whatever colour the background is.

5.3 Using Boolean logic

Boolean logic

We have explored how nested selection statements can be used to make rules more robust, and learned how the AND, OR and NOT Boolean operators can be used in combination with selection statements to reduce the amount of code needed, organise code more effectively and allow our robots to appear more intelligent and dynamic. Now we are going to explore how to combine these Boolean operators and use **Boolean logic** to further refine the code.

Consider this scenario:

Pixie the robot will go to a concert if either Tin Head or Chip are going and if her favourite pop artists – Dot Matrix and Ink Jet – are playing.

> ### Key Term
>
> **Boolean logic**: A form of algebra where all the answers can be reduced to true or false.

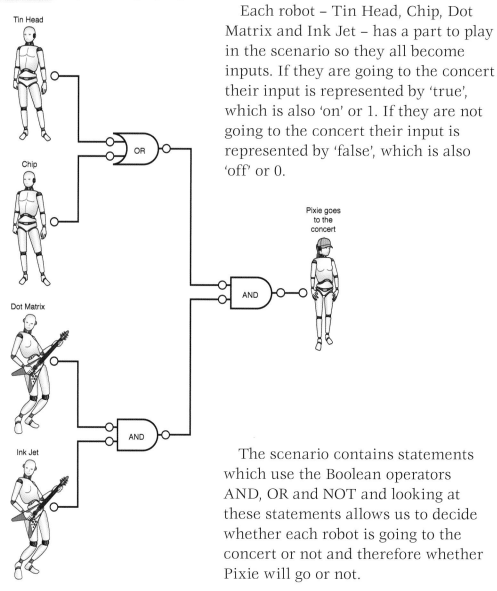

Each robot – Tin Head, Chip, Dot Matrix and Ink Jet – has a part to play in the scenario so they all become inputs. If they are going to the concert their input is represented by 'true', which is also 'on' or 1. If they are not going to the concert their input is represented by 'false', which is also 'off' or 0.

The scenario contains statements which use the Boolean operators AND, OR and NOT and looking at these statements allows us to decide whether each robot is going to the concert or not and therefore whether Pixie will go or not.

Tin Head, Dot Matrix and Ink Jet are all going to the concert so their inputs are 'true' and are switched on. The criteria for Pixie going to the concert have been met so the light bulb is switched on; the result is 'true'.

It would be very time consuming to draw diagrams like this to consider every possible combination of people attending the concert to work out which combinations would result in Pixie also attending. It is much quicker to construct a table. This truth table shows all the possible input combinations and the resulting output.

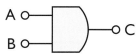
▲ The AND gate output is 'true' if both the inputs are true.

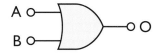
▲ The OR gate output is 'true' if any of the inputs are true.

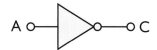
▲ The NOT gate reverses the input, so if the input is false then the output is 'true' and if the input is true then the output is 'false'.

Think-IT

5.3.1   Copy the table below and complete the last column.

Tin Head	Chip	Dot Matrix	Ink Jet	Tin Head OR Chip	Dot Matrix AND Ink Jet	Pixie goes to the concert?
0	0	0	0	0	0	0
0	0	0	1	0	0	0
0	0	1	0	0	0	0
0	0	1	1	0	1	0
0	1	0	0	1	0	0
0	1	0	1	1	0	0
0	1	1	0	1	0	0
0	1	1	1	1	1	1
1	0	0	0	1	0	0
1	0	0	1	1	0	
1	0	1	0	1	0	
1	0	1	1	1	1	
1	1	0	0	1	0	
1	1	0	1	1	0	
1	1	1	0	1	0	
1	1	1	1	1	1	

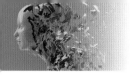

Replacing nested selection statements

As you know, nesting 'if' statements requires lots of code and can make a program difficult to debug and inefficient. However, if we replace nested 'if' selection statements with 'if and' selection statements we can reduce the number of nested 'if' statements and simplify the code.

Compute-IT

5.3.2 a) Adjust the program you created for 5.2.7 Compute-IT, replacing all the nested 'if' selection statements with 'if and' statements.

b) Run and debug your code to ensure that the robot behaves in exactly the same way as it did when your program used nested 'if' selection statements.

Yet it is not always appropriate to use 'if and' selection statements.

Think-IT

5.3.3 Using the knowledge gained from completing 5.3.2 Compute-IT, identify:

a) the advantages and disadvantages of using nested 'if' selection statements

b) the advantages and disadvantages of using 'if and' selection statements.

Reduce processing further with 'if else' selection statements

If a program contains 'if' and 'if and' statements, it has to check against each 'if' or each 'if and' every time the program is run. But, if an '**if else**' statement is used the program does not have to check an input against every single 'if' or 'if and' statement; 'if else' offers you two different routes after a statement or a question.

For example the grades for a test might be awarded according to the following grade boundaries:

Grade A: more than 70
Grade B: 61–70
Grade C: less than 60.

Key Term

if else: Offers two routes after a statement or question.

We can write this as:

`IF greater than 70 THEN 'A' ELSE IF less than 60`
`THEN 'C' ELSE 'B'`

Or we can draw it as a diagram:

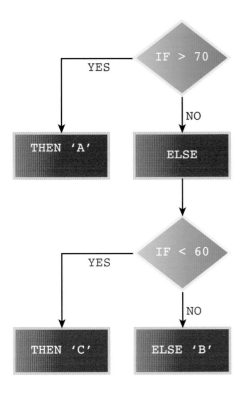

In Scratch 2.0 the program looks like this:

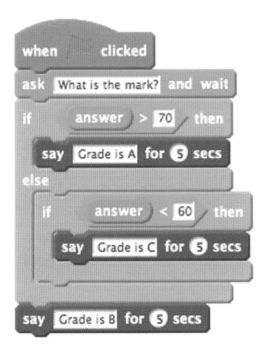

Plan-IT

5.3.4 Draw a flowchart to represent the following scenario:

An online clothing retailer will post orders over £100 free of charge. For orders over £50 they charge £2.99 for postage and packing, otherwise they charge £5.99.

Think-IT

5.3.5 Imagine that someone has thought of a number between 1 and 100. They ask you to guess what that number is and will tell you if you are too high, too low or correct. How would you create a program that guessed the number using 'if else' statements?

Compute-IT

5.3.6 **a)** Modify the program you created for 5.3.2 Compute-IT to include 'if else' selection statements.

b) How many 'if' and 'if and' selection statements did you remove from the program?

5.4 Saving time using loops

Loops and drawing

Using 'if else' selection statements makes code more efficient. Adding repeats, or **loops**, to selection statements allows you to create programs that reuse lines of code, further improving the efficiency of a program. The programmer has less code to input and making adjustments and debugging becomes easier.

Look at the code for drawing a square in Scratch 2.0:

The third and fourth lines of code are repeated four times and if you needed to amend the code to make the square bigger you would need to adjust four lines of code. You would need to change four times.

Key Term

Loop: Also known as a repeat, a loop is a statement that allows a section of code to be executed a number of times.

```
when      clicked
pen down
move 200 steps
turn ↻ 90 degrees
move 200 steps
turn ↻ 90 degrees
move 200 steps
turn ↻ 90 degrees
move 200 steps
turn ↻ 90 degrees
```

```
move 200 steps   to   move 400 steps
```

However, if you use the repeat command to add a loop you can make the code more efficient.

```
when      clicked
pen down
repeat 4
  move 200 steps
  turn ↻ 90 degrees
```

Compute-IT

5.4.1 Modify the program you created for 4.2.2 Compute-IT to include repeat commands to reduce the amount of code.

Different types of loop

Loops can be written in a variety of ways, including:

- **Repeat *n* times**, where *n* is the number of times that a piece of code inside the loop is executed
- **Repeat until**, where code will be repeated inside the loop statement until a variable has a specific value or until the user carries out a specific action
- **Repeat forever**, where the loop continues to repeat until the program is stopped.

Think again about our robot navigating around a maze. It is possible to improve the program using loops. By placing the code within a loop it will no longer be necessary to press the space bar to execute each move the robot makes. Using a repeat command will also enable us to program the robot to move less than a square at a time, making the robot's movements appear smoother and more life-like.

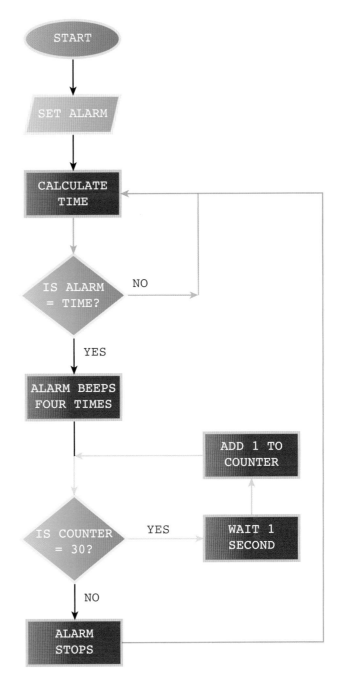

▲ A flowchart of an alarm clock showing three types of loop: blue = repeat *n* times, green = repeat until, red = repeat forever

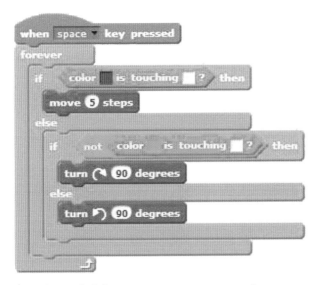

▲ A Scratch 2.0 program using a repeat forever loop to improve the robot program

Think-IT

5.4.2 Explain how you would use a loop to stop your robot when it reaches the end of the maze.

Compute-IT

5.4.3 **a)** Amend the program you created for 5.3.6 Compute-IT, adding a suitable loop so that your robot moves around the maze with a single input, such as a press of the space bar.

b) Increase and decrease the number of steps in the 'move' block. What happens?

Think-IT

5.4.5 What has 5.4.4 Think-IT taught you it is wise to do when programming loops?

Think-IT

5.4.4 What will happen when these pieces of code are executed?

a)   X = 10

Repeat until X < 10

X = X + 1

End Repeat

b) Repeat until X = 500

X = X * 2

End Repeat

c)   X = 100

Repeat until X = 0

X = X / 2

End Repeat

d)   X = 1

Repeat until X = 50

X = X + 3

End Repeat

5.5 Developing algorithms to solve problems

Reintroducing algorithms

A fundamental part of being a computer scientist is being able to solve problems. As we have worked through this unit, we have developed our code to tackle issues as they arise. Now we are going to examine how we can design algorithms that work in a range of different scenarios right from the outset, because creating an efficient **algorithm** before you begin working on writing code usually results in more efficient code. **Programming** bridges the gap between algorithms and computers.

Mazes and algorithms

When we think of mazes, we might think of computer games we play on various types of computer and, indeed, maze computer games have been around since the 1970s. However, mazes have intrigued and entertained people for hundreds of years and the oldest surviving maze in Britain is at Hampton Court Palace.

Key Terms

Algorithm: A series of discrete steps in a particular sequence that can be used to solve a problem.

Programming: The process of writing sequences of instructions that can be interpreted and executed by a computer.

▲ Hampton Court Maze, which has a symmetrical design

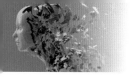
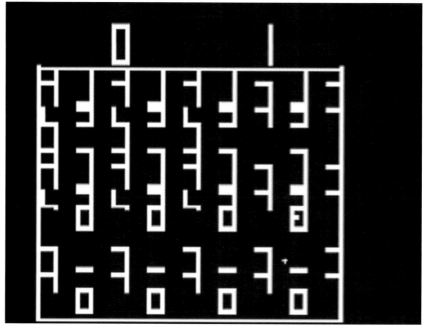

▲ Gotcha! An early maze computer game for two players

Think-IT

5.5.1 This is a plan of Chevening House Maze.

    a) Work your way to the centre.

    b) What approach did you use to reach the centre of the maze?

    c) Now try to reach the centre using the following algorithm. It is called the Random Mouse algorithm.

> **If at junction toss coin**
> **If heads turn left**
> **Else turn right**

    d) Which method of navigating the maze do you think is best, your method or the Random Mouse algorithm? Explain your answer.

Using an algorithm to find a route through a maze is more efficient than trial and error, which is probably what you used to work through the maze the first time. Here is another algorithm, called the Wall Follower:

Check to see if the blue sensor senses the wall

If the blue sensor senses the wall and the pink sensor senses the path, move forwards

If the blue sensor senses the wall and the pink sensor does not sense the path, turn left

If the blue sensor does not sense the wall, turn right

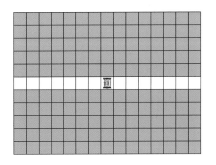

Compute-IT

5.5.2 Using the Wall Follower algorithm write a program for a robot so that it follows the right-hand side of the wall of a maze.

When you know the layout of a maze you can write a purpose-built program that navigates a robot to the centre using a minimal number of instructions. A purpose-built algorithm will probably get your robot to the centre more quickly than the Random Mouse algorithm or the Wall Follower algorithm. However if you try to use your purpose-built algorithm in another maze, with a different layout, you are unlikely to reach the centre. In contrast, the Random Mouse and Wall Follower algorithms may be a bit slower but they will work in any maze; they can be reused.

Often, teams of programmers create a library of algorithms that they share. Whenever a programmer comes across a problem they know someone else has already written an algorithm to solve, they can drag it into place. Once in place the algorithm can be developed and the new, more complex algorithm can become part of the library for someone else to use in the future. It saves programmers having to reinvent the wheel all the time!

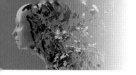

5.6 Adapting algorithms using procedures

Solving exceptions to a problem

Using procedures allows us to take a ready-made algorithm and adapt it to solve similar but slightly different problems. This is an example of computational thinking at work. Pattern recognition is used to identify the similarities and differences between the problem the algorithm was originally written to solve and the current problem, leading to generalisation where the same algorithm is used to solve both problems.

This is a map of six towns – Town A, Town B, Town C, Town D, Town E and Town F – and the railway lines that connect them.

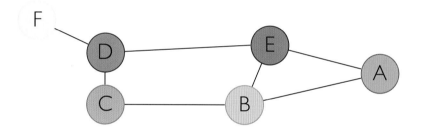

If you are travelling by train you can take a number of different routes between the towns. For example:
You could travel from A to B to C to D to F or you could travel from A to E to D to F and so on.

Think-IT

5.6.1 Write down all the different routes you can take to travel by train from Town A to Town F, passing through each station only once.

Key Term

Path finding: The process of identifying the best route to your destination, according to a set of criteria, using an algorithm.

Path finding is the name given to the process of identifying the best route to your destination using an algorithm. 'Best' can mean quickest or slowest or cheapest, or whatever other criterion is considered most important. Here 'best' is going to mean quickest.

The times in hours between the railway stations in each town are given in the table below.

	A	B	C	D	E	F
A		8			6	
B	8		8		2	
C		8		1		
D			1		10	3
E	6	2		10		
F				3		

Plan-IT

5.6.2 For each of the routes you identified in 5.6.1 Think-IT, work out how long it would take to travel from Town A to Town F.

Compute-IT

5.6.3 a) Which route between Town A and Town F is the best route?

b) Devise an algorithm to identify the best route.

c) What happens if the railway line between Town D and Town E is flooded? Can your algorithm cope with this unexpected circumstance and tell which route is now the best route?

When you are creating algorithms, you need to consider how they will respond to circumstances you can reasonably be expected to foresee as well as unexpected circumstances, particularly problems that emerge during testing.

Adapt by using procedures

Using 'if' selection statements allows us to write an algorithm that responds to different circumstances. For example:

```
IF the railway line between two towns is
  disrupted, THEN seek the next best route.
```

```
IF the station at the town you wish to board the
  train is closed, THEN travel to the next town on
  the route by bus.
```

Key Term

Procedure: A procedure is a section of code that can be used over and over again, which the main program calls on when it needs it. A procedure can accept input from other parts of the program.

However, if you foresee lots of different situations your algorithm will need to respond to it will quickly become very complicated and difficult to debug as a result. In this situation it is a good idea to create a **procedure**. A procedure is another algorithm, a self-contained section of code that the main program can call on when it needs it. You can illustrate a procedure using a flowchart, where 'if' statements are used to establish whether or not the situation the procedure is designed for has happened.

▼ A flowchart showing the Wall Follower algorithm calling a 'Sleep' procedure if another robot, which is travelling at a slower pace, is in the maze

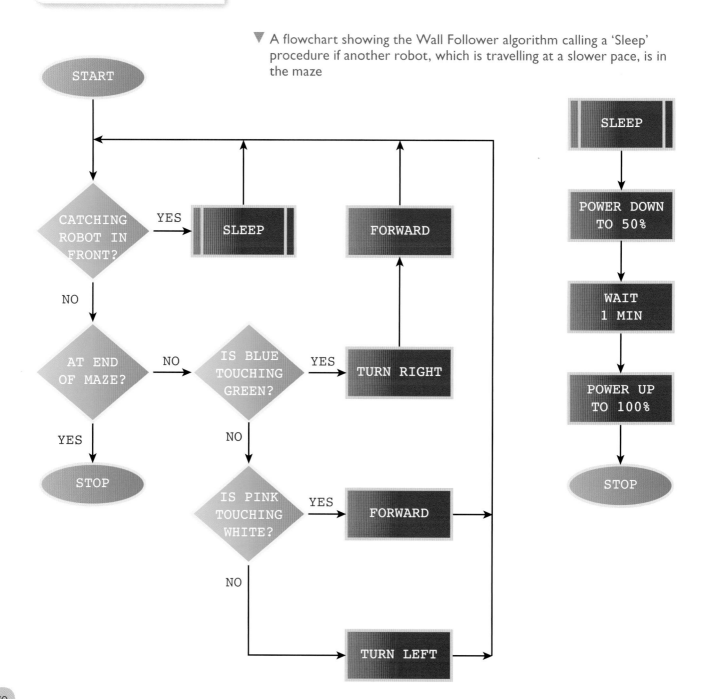

Challenge

Do you remember the challenge for this unit? You have to program a robot that appears to be intelligent; a robot that can successfully navigate around a maze all by itself.

Plan-IT

5.6.4 Design:

- a maze with a multi-coloured background
- a robot with three sensors
- one traffic light sprite to place in your maze. This sprite should have two different costumes, one red and one green, and it should switch between the two costumes every five seconds.

Plan-IT

5.6.5 Draw a flowchart for an algorithm, with procedures where appropriate, which allows your robot to navigate the maze when a key is pressed. Add a procedure so that your robot waits at the traffic lights when they are set to red.

Compute-IT

5.6.6 Program your algorithm, reusing code you have already developed where appropriate.

> You will need to add a new global variable, set for all sprites, called 'Light'. Your robot should move through the traffic light if the variable Light is green or '1' and stop if the variable Light is red or '0'. You learned how to create a variable for the challenge in Unit 4.

Challenge

Your challenge is to split a message into data packets similar to the TCP/IP protocol.

6.1 Internet hardware

How digital devices used to connect to the internet

Most homes in more economically developed countries have a number of electronic devices – smartphones, tablet computers, video game consoles and e-readers, for example – that have the ability to connect and communicate with one another so we can exchange information, transfer files and stream media. We also rely on internet services to stay in touch with friends and family and to navigate the world wide web.

Connecting the home to the internet

When homes first started getting access to the internet they used a dial-up connection, accessing an Internet Service Provider (ISP) via a Public Switch Telephone Network (PSTN) using a telephone line. You had to pay per minute to connect to the internet and you couldn't make phone calls whilst on the internet. The computer was connected to the telephone line via a modem that was used to convert digital information into analogue. Dial-up modems had a much lower bitrate than you get with today's high-speed internet. Theoretically, the average dial-up modem had a transfer speed of 56 KB per second, but in reality connection speeds were much lower and often as low as 20 KB per second.

Dial-up modems were not combined with routers. This meant that if more than one computer wanted to connect to the internet at the same time, a router was required. A router is a device that forwards packets of data along a network and connects two or more networks together.

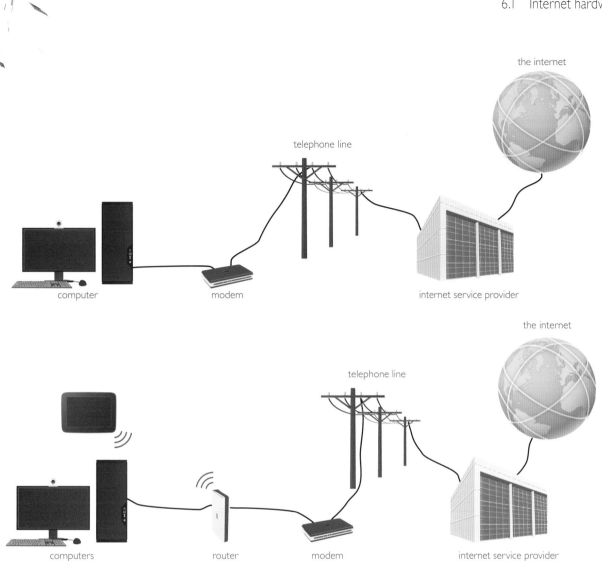

▲ A dial-up connection to the internet, with and without a router. A dial-up modem makes a very particular sound when it is trying to establish a connection to an ISP.

Think-IT

6.1.1 **a)** How many bits could you transfer per second using a 56Kb per second dial-up modem?

b) How many bytes could you transfer per second using a 56Kb per second dial-up modem?

c) How long would it take to transfer a 28.8 KB file using a 56Kb per second dial-up modem?

d) How long would it take to transfer a 9.6 KB file using a 56Kb per second dial-up modem?

e) How long would it take to transfer a 2 MB file using a 56Kb per second dial-up modem?

HINT: Think back to Compute-IT 1 where you learned about file size. There are 8 bits in 1 byte. 1Kb per second is equal to 1024 bits per second or 128 bytes per second. Note we use 'B' for byte and 'b' for bit.

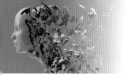
Key Term

Bandwidth: The amount of data that can be transferred from one point to another in a given time period.

Think-IT

6.1.2 Can you think of any internet users who will not like the fact that ADSL has been adjusted so that it is faster to download than it is to upload?

How digital devices connect to the internet today

Fortunately, internet connection speeds are much quicker today. This is because most people connect to the internet using an Asymmetric Digital Subscriber Line or ADSL for short. ADSL is often referred to as broadband. ADSL provides faster transmission of data over copper telephone lines than traditional dial-up modems because it uses a different frequency from the frequency used to make telephone calls, which was the frequency used by dial-up modems. Just like a wider road will hold more cars, a wide frequency telephone line can carry more signals at once, increasing **bandwidth**. And, because your telephone uses a different frequency from your router you can make telephone calls at the same time as using the internet.

The average internet user consumes rather than creates data; they download more than they upload. Uploading is often limited to sending emails, sending requests to see websites and entering logins. The frequency and the carrying capacity of ADSL has therefore been adjusted so it has more downstream capacity and less upstream capacity. That is, there is more capacity for downloading and less capacity for uploading. The difference is often as great as 10:1, reflecting most people's internet usage.

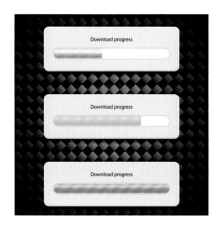

Think-IT

6.1.3 **a)** How many bits could you transfer per second using an 8 Mb per second ADSL connection to the internet?

b) How many bytes could you transfer per second using an 8 Mb per second ADSL connection to the internet?

c) How long would it take to transfer a 28.8 KB file using an 8 Mb per second ADSL connection to the internet?

d) How long would it take to transfer a 9.6 KB file using an 8 Mb per second ADSL connection to the internet?

e) How long would it take to transfer a 2 MB file using an 8 Mb per second ADSL connection to the internet?

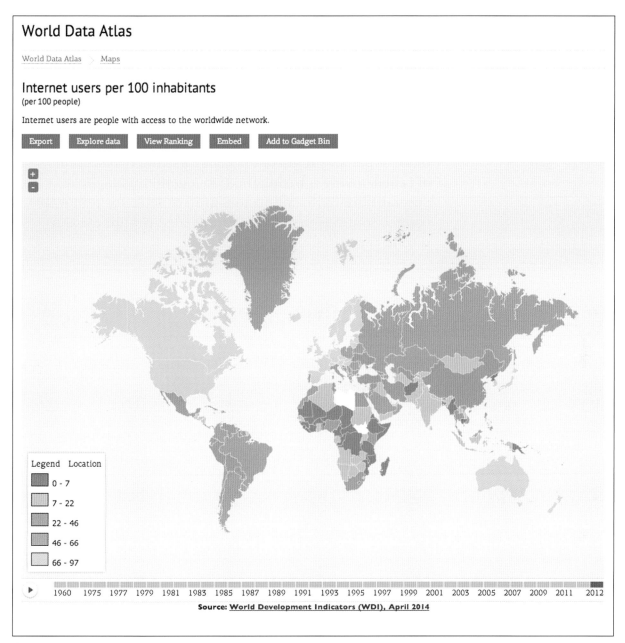

World Data Atlas

World Data Atlas > Maps

Internet users per 100 inhabitants
(per 100 people)

Internet users are people with access to the worldwide network.

| Export | Explore data | View Ranking | Embed | Add to Gadget Bin |

Legend Location

- 0 - 7
- 7 - 22
- 22 - 46
- 46 - 66
- 66 - 97

1960 1975 1977 1979 1981 1983 1985 1987 1989 1991 1993 1995 1997 1999 2001 2003 2005 2007 2009 2011 2012

Source: World Development Indicators (WDI), April 2014

▲ This maps shows the number of people who have access to the internet per 100 inhabitants in 2012.

Unfortunately, some telephone exchanges are not equipped to offer broadband. Recently, the last provider of a dial-up internet connection, BT, switched off the service, leaving some people without access to the internet until they get an ADSL connection.

How digital devices will connect to the internet tomorrow

The fastest broadband is supplied by fibre-optic cables.

Optical fibres are extruded glass or plastic fibres that are thinner than a human hair. Data is passed along these fibres using light.

▲ A fibre-optic cable

Optical fibres have several advantages over copper wires. Data is transferred much more quickly, typically 10 to 40 GB per second. Each individual fibre can carry several channels, each using a different wavelength of light. The signal can also travel much further without needing to be boosted, typically 1,000 metres, compared to the 100 metres for copper cable. Fibre-optic cables are, however, more expensive to install because joining two sections of cables involves fusing the two together using heat. Special fibre-optic connectors are available for removable connections but the equipment needed to capture and resend the signal is quite expensive.

Think-IT

6.1.4 Is access to the internet a human right?

Plan-IT

6.1.5 Carry out research into fibre-optic broadband and answer the following questions.

a) Who provides it?

b) What is the average upstream and downstream capacity?

c) How much does it cost?

d) Is it available in your area?

Key Terms

Local Area Network (LAN): A network of digital devices located in a small geographical area, like a home, school or office building.

Wide Area Network (WAN): A network of digital devices located over a relatively large geographical area. A WAN often consists of many LANs.

Networks

A **Local Area Network**, or **LAN**, is a network of digital devices located in a small geographical area, like a home, a school or an office building. Devices can connect to a LAN using wires or wirelessly and, as part of a LAN, several computers can connect to the same printer for example. Some companies maintain a LAN that is not connected to the internet, mostly for security reasons. Such networks are called intranets. Your school probably has one.

A **Wide Area Network**, or **WAN**, is a network of digital devices that are connected over a relatively large geographical area. A WAN often consists of many LANs joined together using routers. Electrical signals get weaker as they move through a cable, so they need to be re-amplified by a router before being sent on. This makes a WAN more complicated and more expensive than a LAN. The internet is the largest WAN in existence.

Your computer or mobile device has a Network Interface Card, or NIC, that allows it to exchange information with other digital devices. An NIC can take many forms and, nowadays, is probably not actually a card even though the term, a legacy from older technology, is still used. Early computers did not have a case or a keyboard. Instead they had a number of racks where different parts of the computer, such as the memory and processors, were inserted. If a part failed or needed to be upgraded, the old card could be removed from the rack and replaced with a new one.

Wired Ethernet

A Local Area Network can use a protocol called Ethernet to connect devices together. Computers in your school are probably wired via Ethernet, with each computer and printer connected to the network with an Ethernet cable that allows very fast data transfer. Ethernet connections are shared and no computer has exclusive access. Instead, computers communicate in bursts of data called 'frames'.

Wireless Ethernet

Alternatively, digital devices can connect to a LAN using a wifi connection. In this case, both the NIC and the router will usually have a radio antenna that sends out the same Ethernet signals as it would over the wires.

Wifi is slower and less secure than cabled Ethernet but it is still reasonably fast, with connection speeds of up to 600 MB per second. It is also cheaper to set up than cabled Ethernet because there is no need to install expensive cabling. A wifi network is also more useful than a wired network for laptops, tablets and other devices that you want to move around with. However, the further you move from the router, the weaker the signal will be, slowing down data transfer. The quality and age of the router, the materials that walls and furniture are made from and interference from other devices can all affect the speed of a wifi connection. For example, having a regular cordless telephone could slow down your wifi network because cordless telephones can broadcast on the same frequency as wifi antennas. If this happens to you, it should be possible to set your cordless phone and your wifi router to different frequencies.

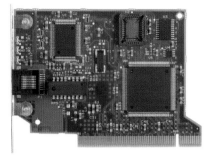

▲ As computer technology becomes physically smaller and the cost of parts goes down, hardware such as NICs are reduced to a small microchip or even integrated into a microchip that carries out many other functions as well.

▲ An Ethernet cable

Wifi networks can be:

- private, such as the one you may have at home
- public, such as the wifi hotspots available in cafes or shopping centres
- mobile, such as GPRS (3G) or 4G. GPRS (General Packet Radio Service) is capable of delivering up to 56 Kb per second data transfer speeds similar to a dial-up modem. It is particularly good for sending and receiving short bursts of data such as email, but cannot deal with large volumes of data. 3G (third generation) is a wide area cell-based standard for mobile communication capable of transfer speeds up to 21 Mb per second. 4G (fourth generation) integrates the wide area cell-based mobile system with wifi to deliver even greater data transfer speeds up to 100 Mb per second.

Your digital device will search for wifi networks. Each network will have a name, known as an SSID or Service Set Identifier, and most will require a password to gain access. All devices connected to an SSID are on the same network and can exchange data. This can be potentially dangerous. Hackers can lure people onto wifi networks by offering free internet access and, once connected, can access their files. This is why it is important to have a firewall in place. A firewall is used to protect a device and/or a network from unauthorised access from outside.

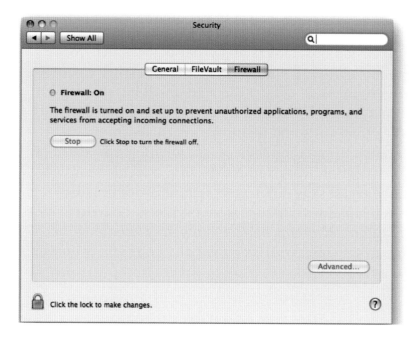

Turning on the firewall for a device provides protection from applications, programs and services gaining unauthorised access through incoming connections. ▶

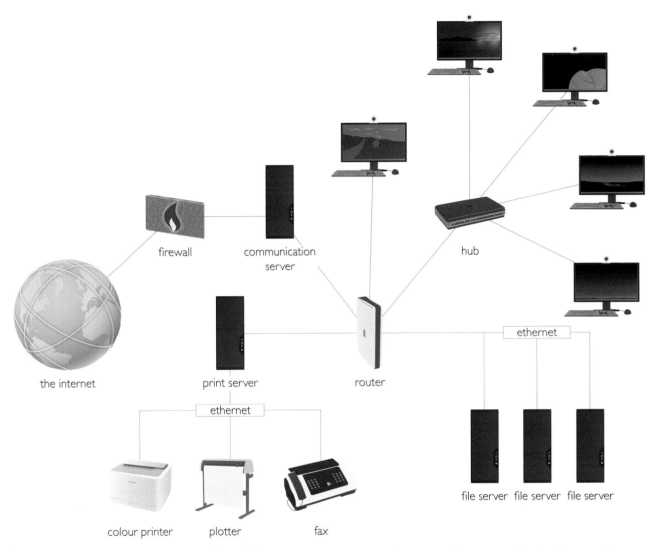

▲ A firewall sits between a network and the internet to protect the system from unauthorised access from outside the LAN.

Think-IT

6.1.6 **a)** Connect to a website that provides details of your internet connection speed using a mobile digital device. In a spreadsheet, record the upload and download speeds of your connection when you connect to the internet via a private wifi network, a public wifi network and a 3G network.

b) Next, record the speed of your connection when you connect to the internet using a desktop computer in school and, if you have a computer at home, at home.

c) Sort the data by download speeds and then by upload speeds. What do you notice?

Key Term

Internet Service Provider (ISP): A company that provides access to internet services.

Internet Service Providers

An **Internet Service Provider (ISP)** connects a LAN to the internet, which is a WAN.

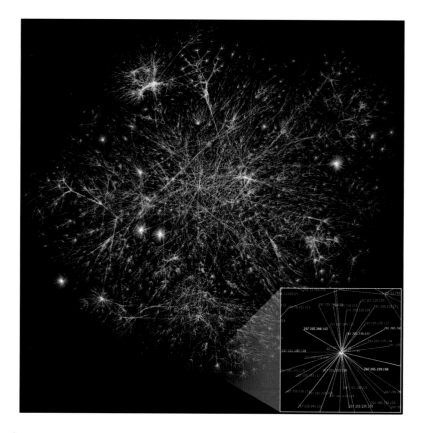

This is a partial map of the internet. Each line connects two devices. How does your computer know how to navigate this? ▶

There are many ISPs and they offer a range of different internet services. When selecting your ISP you should consider these points:

- **The cost:** Faster speeds and higher download limits cost more.
- **Speed:** Both the maximum download and upload speeds.
- **Type of connection:** Fibre-optic cables offer faster speeds than copper cables. Do the cables your connection will use support the maximum speeds your ISP promises?
- **Download limits:** Many ISPs offer unlimited downloads but some have fair usage policies to enable them to limit excessive downloads if this is likely to affect others who share the connection.
- **Reliability and customer service.**
- **Email services:** Most, but not all, ISPs provide email services. Some limit the number of email addresses provided.

- Hosting service: Many ISPs will provide a hosting service for storing your most important files. Some also provide you with the option of creating and managing your own website.
- Wifi hotspots: Some providers offer access to wifi hotspots so you can access the internet while you are away from home.

Think-IT

6.1.7 **a)** What is the name of the ISP that provides your internet at home and what services does it provide?

b) Consider the list of services an ISP can provide above and list them in your own personal order of priority.

c) Compare the service you receive from your ISP with your personal priorities. Are you getting value for money?

d) Given the choice, would you change your ISP? Justify your decision.

Think-IT

6.1.8 **a)** Create the following table in a spreadsheet and then complete it:

	A	B	C	D
1	**The places I connect to the internet** For example, home, a café, a friend's house, school and a bus or railway station	**Type of connection** For example, wired, private wifi, public wifi hotspot, mobile wifi (GPRS, 3G or 4G)	**The average number of minutes I spend connected to the internet in this location each week**	
2				
3				
4				
5				
6				
7				

b) Using your table:

i) work out where you connect to the internet most often and where you connect to the internet least often

ii) work out the total time you spend connected to the internet each week for each type of connection.

c) Using data gathered from other students:

i) work out the most popular and least popular places to connect to the internet

ii) work out the most popular and least popular type of connection used to connect to the internet.

d) Compare your internet usage from part b with your findings for part c.

6.2 Internet protocol: TCP/IP

Packets of data

As you have already learned, computers communicate via a continuous stream of zeros and ones, but how do those zeros and ones travel from source to destination?

The computers on your LAN have local addresses and communicate with each other directly by sending their messages, split into Physical Data Units (PDUs), around the network. PDUs are also called 'frames' or 'packets'. The router notices any packets destined for IP addresses outside the LAN, scoops them up and sends them to the wider network, hoping that all the other routers on the internet will work out how to deliver them to their final destination. This is known as a default gateway. These packets then take different routes to get to their destinations, often many thousands of kilometres away, and some will sadly never make it.

Compute-IT

6.2.1

a) Look at a map of the London Underground network. Select a starting point for your journey and select a destination. Your starting point and destination can be anywhere on the map.

b) Write down the journey you would take to travel from your chosen starting point to your destination.

c) Ask a partner to put a blockage on the line somewhere along the route you wrote down for part b. Can you still get to your destination? If not, what should you do? Write down your new route to your destination.

d) If secret service agents wanted to transfer confidential information from Euston Square to Old Street they might split the information into several different pieces and use a number of different agents, each carrying a different piece and travelling on a different route, to get the information to its destination. What are the advantages of this?

The output of software applications, such as file downloaders or email clients, gets split into standard-sized packets before it is sent through the network. If the output is too small to fit into a standard-sized packet, the router will pad out the packet with extra zeros.

The router packs each packet into an 'envelope'. Parts of the envelope, called headers and trailers, contain **metadata** about the data being sent, which includes:

> **Key Term**
>
> **Metadata**: Data about data.

- the source address and the destination address for the data
- the expiry time (if packets do not arrive at their destination after a certain amount of time, they are deleted)
- the serial number of the packet so the full output can be reassembled correctly when it reaches its destination
- recovery and error checking data (extra data that can be used to check if the packet has become corrupted on its journey)
- information about the software that generated the data.

As this packet travels to its destination, it is put inside more envelopes. Rules, or 'protocols', define how each packet is packed in a series of envelopes so they can be unpacked in the correct order at their destination. These protocols are called TCP/IP (Transmission Control Protocol/Internet Protocol).

▲ As each packet travels to its destination, it is put inside more envelopes, rather like the smallest doll in a Russian stacking doll is put inside the larger dolls.

Think-IT

6.2.2 A simple way to communicate in a small room is to write a message on a mini-whiteboard and hold it up for someone to see. If you were sending the message in a room full of people you would have to include some method for identifying the intended recipient. If they were not in line of sight you would have to ask others to relay the message and you would want some way of acknowledging the message was received. Design a set of protocols for sending messages in this way.

Circuit switching vs packet switching

As we know, all the packets of data that make up, for example, an email message do not take the same route to their destination. Why not?

In telephone networks and early computer networks, data was not divided into packets. A path, or connection, between two computers that wanted to communicate with each other was established before data was sent. This is called **circuit switching**, where a dedicated circuit between intermediate nodes (or switches) forms a connection that is maintained for the duration of the required data transmission (or call). All data between the two computers follows the same route. An advantage of this is that a guaranteed bandwidth can be reserved, which is why it is good for telephone calls. However, this does mean that the reserved circuit of the network is not available for use by other users, which can lead to users waiting for a connection over the same area of the network, or to wasted bandwidth if more bandwidth is reserved than is actually required for the data to be communicated. Also, if the established route is subject to disruption, then the whole connection can be lost. Finally, if the circuits are known, then it is relatively easy to eavesdrop a complete communication between the two computers, and, in particular, to eavesdrop two-way communication.

> **Key Term**
>
> **Circuit switching**: A data transfer method where a single path is created between sender and receiver.

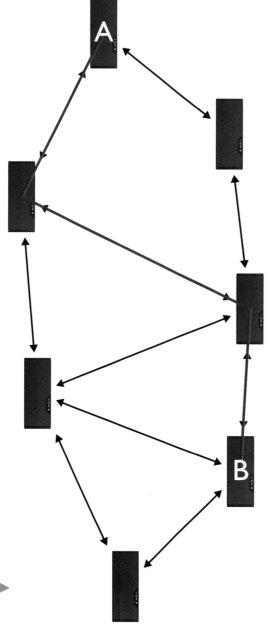

Circuit switching: a circuit is opened and maintained between A and B for the duration of the data transfer ▶

By splitting data into packets and allowing them to find their own way to their destination, the **packet switching** approach overcomes the weaknesses of the circuit switching approach. Unavailable or congested circuits can be avoided, packets from different data streams and between different users can share parts of the same route, and lost or damaged packets can be resent (and can take different routes to the destination). All along the route, the packets are helped by routers. Routers communicate with each other and contain shortest-path calculators, so the advice they provide to the packets that pass through them is not just about which route to take but also about the traffic conditions along that route. The fact that no dedicated circuit is reserved to establish a connection between the two end points also means that interception is harder; packets on different routes have to be intercepted and reassembled and packets from a two-way communication can take completely different routes over the network.

Key Term

Packet switching: A data transfer method where data is split into packets and each packet finds its own route from sender to receiver.

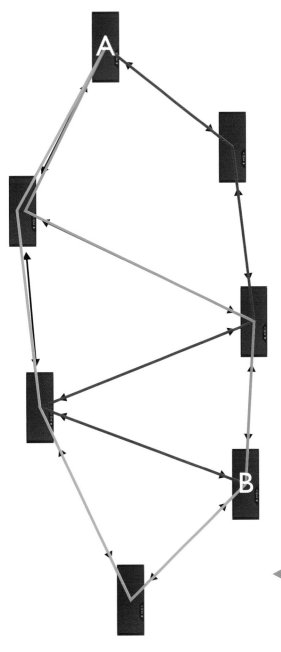

◀ Packet switching: Data is split into packets and takes various routes through the network from A to B

IP addresses

Ethernet LANs are not very efficient. They were originally designed for sharing a printer on a local network and do not cope well with the massive flow of data that passes between devices today. They are quite fast when the data flow is small, but if one user on the network is uploading or downloading a large file all the other devices on the network will slow down. This is because packets circulating around an Ethernet LAN are sent to all the devices connected to the network and the device that wants them reaches out and grabs them as they go past.

Unlike an Ethernet LAN, the internet has an address system that ties packets to physical devices. Every device connected to the internet has a unique **IP address**, which is expressed by a series of decimal numbers and dots for humans and in binary for computers.

Key Term

IP address: A number allocated to each digital device on a network to uniquely identify it.

Data is circulated to all connected devices in an Ethernet LAN and the device that wants the data has to grab it as it goes past, just like you have to grab your suitcase or rucksack off the belt at baggage reclaim at an airport. ▶

For a long time we have used an IP standard called IPv4. It is made up of four bytes. Each byte can hold 256 different binary combinations, so each of the four parts of an address is a number between 000 and 255. Between them, the 32 bits of an IP address can have up to 2^{32} or 4,294,967,296 unique values. Some combinations – such as 0000.0000.0000.0000 and 255.255.255.255.255 – are restricted.

The first byte identifies the network and the last byte identifies the device.

123.123.123.123
Byte 1   Byte 2   Byte 3   Byte 4

The maximum number of possible IP addresses sets a limit on the number of devices that can connect to the internet at any given time. As there are more devices in the world that want to connect to the internet than there are IP addresses, most devices are loaned a dynamic IP address for a period of time. Every time a device connects to the internet it receives a different dynamic IP address. Servers are an exception, however. They usually have static IP addresses that do not change.

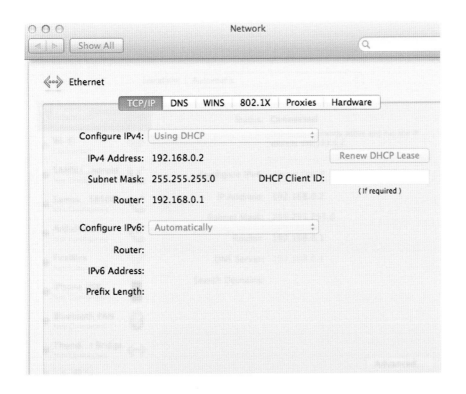

Think-IT

6.2.3 Why can each byte hold 256 different binary combinations?

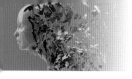

When the internet was first created, all you needed was a computer's IP address to connect to it and, for example, look at one of its web pages. As more and more people started using the internet and the number of machines on the internet increased, the **Domain Name System (DNS)** was created to provide text-based names for machines that mapped to their IP addresses. Given a name, large databases, called domain servers, can look up the corresponding IP address for the machine. The advantages of naming machines include:

- the ability to replace machines yet maintain the same name by changing the name to IP address mapping in the DNS
- the use of well-known names for services (for example, mail.somecompany.org or www. somecompany.org) that are easier for people to remember.

> ### Key Term
>
> **Domain Name System (DNS)**: The name given to the system that converts text-based addresses to IP addresses.

Compute-IT

6.2.4 a) Convert the binary strings below into decimal IPv4 IP addresses. Then type the IP addresses into a web browser and note down the websites they open.

	Binary IPv4 IP address	Decimal IPv4 IP address	Website
1	11011110.00111010.11110110.01011110		
2	10111100.01011100.10001101.00011100		
3	01001010.01111101.11101111.10011000		

Here is a table of the binary column values for an 8-bit binary number to help you.

128	64	32	16	8	4	2	1

For example 11000001 = 128 + 64 + 1 = 193, so the binary IP address 11000001.01111111.00011110.00010111 can be converted as follows:

11000001	01111111	00011110	00010111
193	127	30	23

b) There are online tools that tell you what the IP address for a website is. Type 'what is my IP address' into a search engine and find the tools to convert hostname to IP. Now find out the decimal IPv4 IP address for the following websites and then convert the decimal IP address into a binary IPv4 IP address.

Website	Decimal IPv4 IP address	Binary IPv4 IP address
www.hp.com		
www.microsoft.com		

Subnets

IPv4 provides over four billion IP addresses, but we are running out as the number of digital devices that want to connect to the internet continues to increase. It isn't time to panic though. If we allocate the IP address to a router then we can turn four billion devices into four billion networks. These networks, that appear to be one device to the outside world, are called subnets.

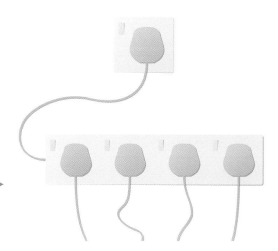

Just as a four-gang extension allows you to power four ▶ different devices from one wall socket, allocating the IP address to a router allows you to connect more than one device to the internet using just one IP address.

Think-IT

6.2.5

```
Received: by 10.216.180.6 with SMTP id i6csp319659wem;
        Thu, 26 Sep 2013 07:51:12 -0700 (PDT)
X-Received: by 10.194.119.132 with SMTP id ku4mr1175367wjb.51.1380207072023;
        Thu, 26 Sep 2013 07:51:12 -0700 (PDT)
Return-Path: <ATL_communications@atlunion.org.uk>
Received: from mail3.marketing.etelligent.co.uk (mail3.marketing.etelligent.co.uk. [80.76.192.114])
        by mx.google.com with ESMTP id jr6si842135wjc.99.1969.12.31.16.00.00;
        Thu, 26 Sep 2013 07:51:12 -0700 (PDT)
Received-SPF: pass (google.com: domain of ATL_communications@atlunion.org.uk designates 80.76.192.114 as
permitted sender) client-ip=80.76.192.114;
Authentication-Results: mx.google.com;
        spf=pass (google.com: domain of ATL_communications@atlunion.org.uk designates 80.76.192.114 as
permitted sender) smtp.mail=ATL_communications@atlunion.org.uk
Received: from mail pickup service by mail3.marketing.etelligent.co.uk with Microsoft SMTPSVC;
        Thu, 26 Sep 2013 15:53:29 +0100
```

▲ This shows a message travelling through various routers on its way to its destination.

Identify the three IP addresses for devices that received this data on its journey.

Compute-IT

6.2.6 a) Search for a 'trace route program' on the internet or use the command line option for your computer's operating system to trace the route taken by a message from your computer to various websites.

b) Look at the routers the message passes through on its way to its destination. Find out where each router is located using the tool you used for 6.2.4b Compute-IT.

c) Use a map to trace the physical route the message took using these locations.

d) Trace the route the message takes to the same location a second time. Does it travel along the same route?

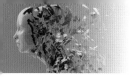
6.3 Layering of protocols

TCP/IP layers

Over the years, two concerns have consistently occupied the people who develop computing technology:

- How do we make sure that data is delivered reliably and if not, then resent if it is corrupted?
- How do we guarantee that all software and all hardware, now or in the future, can accept data from all other software and hardware?

To tackle these problems, data that flows on the internet is constructed in layers, a little like the way in which a pavement is built.

A pavement is built in layers as shown on the right. Data that flows on the internet is also constructed in layers to ensure it reaches its destination reliably. ▶

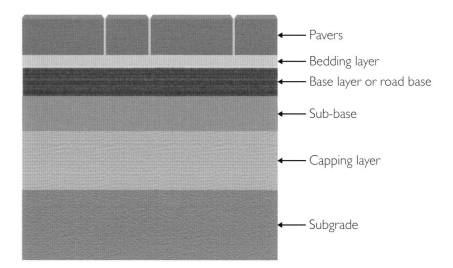

Pavers
Bedding layer
Base layer or road base
Sub-base
Capping layer
Subgrade

There are four layers in the TCP/IP Stack, each made of bits containing zeros and ones. The information contained in each layer is added to the data to be sent as headers and trailers.

Application	010101101101101011011010110101011011001010110110110101101101011010
Door-to-door transport	110101101101101010101011011010110110101101101011010101101101011010110101
Internet	00101011011011010110110101101010110110101101011011010110101101101010110101010
Network	101101011010101101101011101011101101101010101011110101110110110101010101

Let's make sense of all these binary digits!

Layer 1: Application
The data is sent by a software program, such as a web browser or an email client, that communicates with its counterpart software program at the destination. This layer establishes the protocol that will be used by the two programs to communicate. Email clients use protocols such as SMTP or POP or IMAP. Web browsers and servers use a protocol called HTTP. Other protocols that are used in this layer are FTP (File Transfer Protocol), which allows you to transfer files from one computer to another using the internet, and VOIP (Voice Over IP), which carries telephone conversations over the internet.

Layer 2: Door-to-door transport
As soon as the data has had its first layer added, it knocks on the door of the operating system asking to be let out. The operating system splits the data into packets, each numbered so they can be reassembled in the correct order at their destination. It then communicates with the receiving device to find out how fast the sending device can send the data and how fast the receiving device can accept the data. The devices also agree whether the receiving machine will confirm receipt of each packet using the Transmission Control Protocol (TCP) or save time and not confirm receipt of each packet using the more unreliable but faster User Datagram Protocol (UDP).

00101001|01001010|
10101100|11001100|
TCP or UDP?

Layer 3: Internet
Connecting the sending device and the receiving device requires finding out exactly where each of them is on the internet by identifying their IP addresses and the IP addresses of the routers through which the data will pass to travel between them. The port the data will use to leave the sending device and arrive at the receiving device is also identified in this layer. A computer port is a type of electronic post box to which information is posted to your computer from the internet or from another computer in a network.

Layer 4: Network
Independent of other layers, this layer converts the data into electrical signals understood by the second device's network card and LAN so it can be sent to the internet via Ethernet cable or wireless.

00101001|01001010|
10101100|11001100|

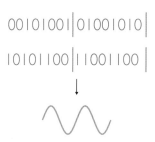

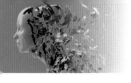

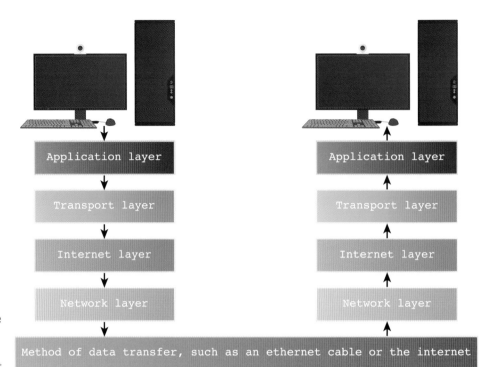

This diagram shows the layers being added to enable a device to send data to another device using the internet. ▶

Data corruption

Some packets never make it to their destination. This can be for several reasons:

- They get lost, following a route to their destination that is a dead end.
- There is a data collision. The packet reaches its destination or one of the routers along its route to its destination at exactly the same time as another packet and is lost.
- The header and trailer data is corrupted, ones turn to zeros and zeros turn to ones.

If the ones and zeros in the body of the data itself become corrupted, it is important that the receiving device identifies this and asks the sending device to resend the packet that has been corrupted. A common way to work out if a packet has been corrupted is for the sending device to add up all the ones it contains and, if the total is odd, set the parity bit to 1 and, if the total is even, set the parity bit to 0. The parity bit is then transmitted as part of the packet. The receiving device then recounts the number of ones and zeros in the packet and identifies the parity bit. If the parity bit set by the sending device and the parity bit set by the receiving device are the same, then the data is not corrupted. If they are different, then something about the data has changed; it has been corrupted.

Compute-IT

6.3.1 Add parity bits to the following 7-bit data items:

    a) 1001000

    b) 1101101

    c) 1010111

    d) 1100110

Compute-IT

6.3.2 Which of the following data items have been corrupted if we are using a parity bit to check for corruption?

    a) 11100111

    b) 11011010

    c) 11111101

    d) 10000001

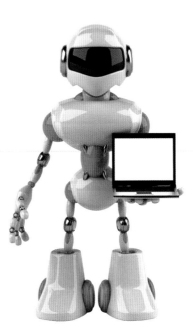

Challenge

Do you remember the challenge at the start of this unit, to send a message to a friend using the TCP/IP protocol?

Compute-IT

6.3.3 Write a very short message, such as 'I like computing', and then simulate the way in which this message would reach a friend if you sent it to them by email. Think about:

■ How your imaginary digital device will connect to the internet. Will your digital device be connected to an Ethernet LAN or a wifi LAN?

■ How you will convert your message into binary and split it into packets.

■ How you will add the metadata for the four layers of the TCP/IP Stack.

Challenge

Your challenge is to write a program for a high-score table for a computer game.

7.1 What are sorting algorithms?

Sorting

We often need to present data in a specific order. Here are a few examples:

	A	B	C	D	E	F	G
1	Region	Jan	Feb	Mar	Apr	May	June
2	Region 01	50	100	100	100	74	100
3	Region 02	35.78	60.85	99.02	110.9	31.94	114.66
4	Region 03	49.03	116.92	37.96	88.9	56.08	62
5	Region 04	9.71	73.4	115.22	122.63	97.33	54.2
6	Region 05	5.11	85.22	98.83	67	72.24	57.79
7	Region 06	124.27	123.77	3.24	101.5	42.39	60.23
8	Region 07	44.75	77.13	125.13	131.17	117.15	41.25
9	Region 08	145.7	62.08	27.54	126.79	70.97	73.32

▲ A spreadsheet

▲ The results of a search for products on a website

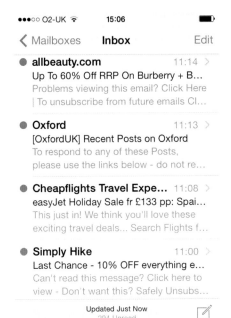

▲ An email inbox

▲ Contacts on a mobile phone

▲ A train departure board

▲ A high-score table for a computer game

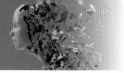

Key Terms

Ascending order: Data that is sorted from the lowest value to the highest value is sorted in ascending order. For example, A to Z and 0 to 9.

Descending order: Data that is sorted from the highest value to the lowest value is sorted in descending order. For example, Z to A and 9 to 0.

Think-IT

7.1.1   Which of the following lists would be easiest to sort into **ascending order**? Which would be easiest to sort into **descending order**?

a) 1, 2, 3, 5, 4, 6

b) 6, 4, 5, 3, 2, 1

c) 4, 2, 6, 5, 1, 3

Think-IT

7.1.2   Sort the following lists into ascending and descending order:

a) Beryl, Emerald, Opal, Amethyst, Diamond, Jade

b) 12, 65, 44, 98, 43.5, 3, 72

Think-IT

7.1.3   A list of names is sorted into ascending order in two different programs. Each program gives a different output. Why?

Program 1: ahmed, Alicia, betsy, Brian, ciaran, Claire, denise, Dev

Program 2: Alicia, Brian, Claire, Dev, ahmed, betsy, ciaran, denise

Compute-IT

7.1.4   Before exploring how to program a sorting algorithm in a graphical programming language we need to be able to put data into a list, so create a list in a graphical programming language and then import a text file.

Computers use sorting to put data into order and, as with anything we want a computer to do, if we want a computer to sort data we need to program it. Sorting programs are based on algorithms. A number of sorting algorithms already exist and the one we choose can depend on the state of data that is going to be sorted, for example, how many items there are or whether they are already partly in order. The choice of algorithm can also depend on how easy it is to program and how efficient it is.

BogoSort and Swap Sort

When thinking about sorting algorithms, one of the most important things to consider is how long the algorithm takes to sort data. Imagine wanting to re-order your emails by date and having to wait 30 seconds!

BogoSort

BogoSort puts all the items in the list into a random order. If they happen to be in a sorted order, we stop. Otherwise we try again.

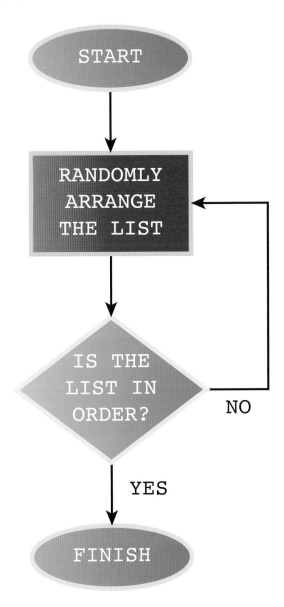

Swap Sort

Swap Sort selects two items in the list at random and swaps them if they are out of order. It repeats this process until all the cards are in order.

Think-IT

7.1.5 Compare BogoSort and Swap Sort. Which is the better sorting algorithm and why?

7.2 Bubble Sort

Bubble Sort is a sorting algorithm. It has a **flag** that tells us that a swap has been made. You can picture this as a person holding a flag, which they raise and lower when told to:

Flag = true =

Flag = false =

In programming, the term 'flag' refers to a Boolean (true/false) variable which can be used to show us if something has happened or if something is available to use.

Let's work through an example:

Bear, Ape, Dog, Fish, Cat, Elk We start with the first item and compare it to the item next to it. As they are not in order we swap them and set the flag to true.	
Ape, Bear, Dog, Fish, Cat, Elk Now we look at the second item. The item in position two is in order with the item in position three, so we move to the next position. The flag stays at true because a swap has previously been made.	
Ape, Bear, Dog, Fish, Cat, Elk Again, the item in position three is in order with the item in position four so we move along. The flag stays at true because a swap has previously been made.	
Ape, Bear, Dog, Fish, Cat, Elk Fish and Cat are out of order so we swap them. If the flag wasn't already showing as true, we would set it to true.	
Ape, Bear, Dog, Cat, Fish, Elk Now we look at the item in the fifth position. Fish and Elk are out of order so we switch them. Again, if the flag wasn't already showing as true, we would set it to true.	
Ape, Bear, Dog, Cat, Elk, Fish The item in position six is at the end of the list. We check to see if the flag is showing true or false. It is showing true. This means that we cannot yet be sure that the list is in order. We can only tell that the list is in order if, when we process the list, no swaps have been made and the flag shows false.	
We therefore reset the flag to false and go back to the beginning. **Ape, Bear, Dog, Cat, Elk, Fish** Dog and Cat are out of order so we swap them and set the flag to true.	

> **Ape, Bear, Cat, Dog, Elk, Fish**
> Again, we are at the end of the list and we need to check the flag. Because we have made a swap the flag is true. Whilst we can see in this example the list is sorted, the computer can't tell this yet. It has to go back to the start and run through the process again. This time, because there won't be any swaps the flag will still be false at the end of the process, showing that the list is now sorted.

We can represent Bubble Sort as a flowchart (see below on the right):

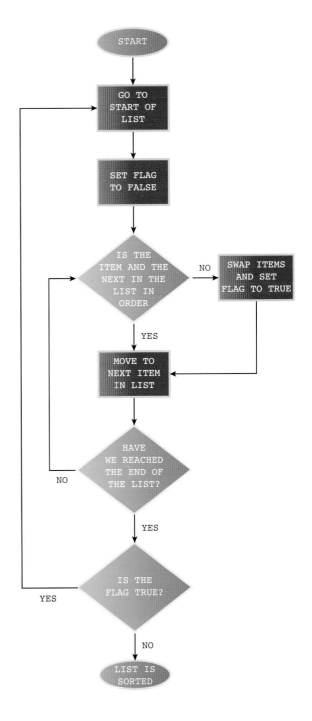

Compute-IT

7.2.1 Sort this list using Bubble Sort, recording each step of the process:

> **Fish, Dog, Elk, Ape, Bear, Cat**

Compute-IT

7.2.2 Sort these two lists using Bubble Sort. Which list will be sorted quickest and why?

> **List A: Bear, Cat, Dog, Elk, Fish, Ape**
> **List B: Fish, Ape, Bear, Cat, Dog, Elk**

Think-IT

7.2.3 Using the internet, find out how you could alter Bubble Sort to overcome the issues you identified when you completed 7.2.2 Compute-IT.

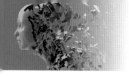

Key Term

Pseudocode: A system of writing resembling a simplified programming language, used in program design.

7.3 Implementing Bubble Sort

Pseudocode

Pseudocode has the structure of a programming language but is designed to be read by a person rather than a computer. It's halfway between a flowchart and code, and it is a useful tool for planning a program. We can write the pseudocode for a sorting algorithm like Bubble Sort and then use it to help us code the program in a graphical programming language.

Writing pseudocode for Bubble Sort

Let's take a look at the key things Bubble Sort needs to be able to do. It needs to be able to:

- move through a list one item at a time
- compare two items
- swap two items.

First it needs to move through a list one item at a time. To do this we need to use a loop or iteration. In pseudocode, this might look like this:

> We only go up to **List. Length–1**, that is, to the last but one item in the list, because there is nothing to compare the last item in the list with.

```
FOR i=1 TO List.Length-1
    Perform comparison
NEXT i
```

> *i* is the position of item being checked in the list. *=1* is the first item in the list. Therefore *i=1* means that the first item being checked in the list is the first item in the list.

> We'll write this bit of the pseudocode in a moment.

As the program moves through the list one item at a time, each item must be compared with the next item. This is done using **IF**.

```
FOR i=1 TO List.Length-1
IF List[i]>List[i+1] THEN
    Swap the items
ENDIF
NEXT i
```

> **>** means 'greater than'.

Think-IT

7.3.1 a) *List[i]* means 'get item number i in the list'. Click on 'Data' on the 'Scripts' tab in Scratch 2.0 and then click on 'Make a List'. Give your list a name and click 'OK'. Which of the code blocks you can now see is equivalent to this?

b) Scratch 2.0 doesn't have a block for **FOR** either. What is its equivalent?

Bubble Sort must swap the items if the first item is greater than the second item. At first sight, swapping two variables seems straightforward. Look at the following example.

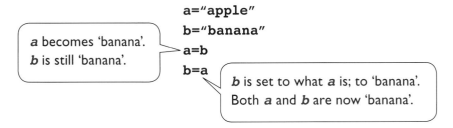

a="apple"
b="banana"
a=b
b=a

a becomes 'banana'.
b is still 'banana'.

b is set to what *a* is; to 'banana'.
Both *a* and *b* are now 'banana'.

Think-IT

7.3.2 Imagine you have two jars, one containing water and one containing orange juice. Swapping the contents of the jars is impossible without a third, empty jar. Using this idea, use a third variable, **c**, to swap the values 'apple' and 'banana' in the code above.

If we want to swap an item in the list with the item that follows it we need an extra variable. We can call this variable **temp**.

```
FOR i=1 TO List.Length-1
    IF List[i]>List[i+1] THEN
            temp=List[i]
            List[i]=List[i+1]
            List[i+1]=temp
    ENDIF
NEXT i
```

The complete Bubble Sort algorithm in pseudocode is therefore:

```
flag=true
WHILE flag=true
    flag=false
    FOR i=1 TO List.Length-1
        IF List[i]>List[i+1] THEN
            temp=List[i]
            List[i]=List[i+1]
            List[i+1]=temp
            flag=true
        ENDIF
    NEXT i
ENDWHILE
```

We set the flag to true before we start so the loop executes at least once.

The loop executes while the flag is set to true.

The flag is set to false before the loop is executed.

If a swap is made the flag is set to true so the loop executes once more.

If no swaps are made, the flag is still set to false and the loop ends.

Compute-IT

7.3.3 Program Bubble Sort in a graphical programming language, using the pseudocode to help you.

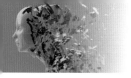

7.4 Selection Sort

Selection Sort

Selection Sort is another sorting algorithm. It finds the smallest item in the list and swaps it with the item in position 1. It then finds the next smallest item and swaps it with the item in position 2. This continues until it gets to the end of the list, by which time the list is sorted.

Let's work through an example:

Cardiff, Aberdeen, Derby, Gloucester, Belfast, Edinburgh

We start with the item in position one and look through the list to find the smallest item.
We swap the smallest item with the item in position one.
We now know that the list is sorted up to position one.

Aberdeen, **Cardiff, Derby, Gloucester, Belfast, Edinburgh**

We now move to position two and, again, find the smallest item in the remaining part of the list and make a swap.

Aberdeen, Cardiff, Derby, Gloucester, Belfast, Edinburgh
Aberdeen, Belfast, **Derby, Gloucester, Cardiff, Edinburgh**

The list is now sorted up to position two. We keep repeating the process until we get to the end of the list.

Aberdeen, Belfast, **Derby, Gloucester, Cardiff, Edinburgh**
Aberdeen, Belfast, Cardiff, **Gloucester, Derby, Edinburgh**
Aberdeen, Belfast, Cardiff, **Gloucester, Derby, Edinburgh**
Aberdeen, Belfast, Cardiff, Derby, **Gloucester, Edinburgh**
Aberdeen, Belfast, Cardiff, Derby, **Gloucester, Edinburgh**
Aberdeen, Belfast, Cardiff, Derby, Edinburgh, **Gloucester**
Aberdeen, Belfast, Cardiff, Derby, Edinburgh, **Gloucester**
Aberdeen, Belfast, Cardiff, Derby, Edinburgh, Gloucester

Plan-IT

7.4.1   Draw a flowchart to show how Selection Sort works.

Compute-IT

7.4.2 Sort this list using Selection Sort, recording each step of the process:

Fish, Dog, Elk, Ape, Bear, Cat

Compute-IT

7.4.3 Sort these two lists using Selection Sort. Predict which list will be sorted quickest and why.

List A: Bear, Cat, Dog, Elk, Fish, Ape

List B: Fish, Ape, Bear, Cat, Dog, Elk

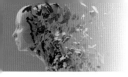

7.5 Implementing Selection Sort

Writing pseudocode for Selection Sort

Selection Sort needs to be able to:

- move through a list one item at a time
- find the smallest item in a list
- swap two items.

We already know how to move through a list one item at a time and swap two items (see section 7.4). To find the smallest item in a list we can use the following algorithm:

```
FOR i=1 TO List.Length
    Find smallest item between item[i] and end
    Swap item[i] with smallest item
NEXT i
```

We need to track the position of the smallest item in the list rather than its value:

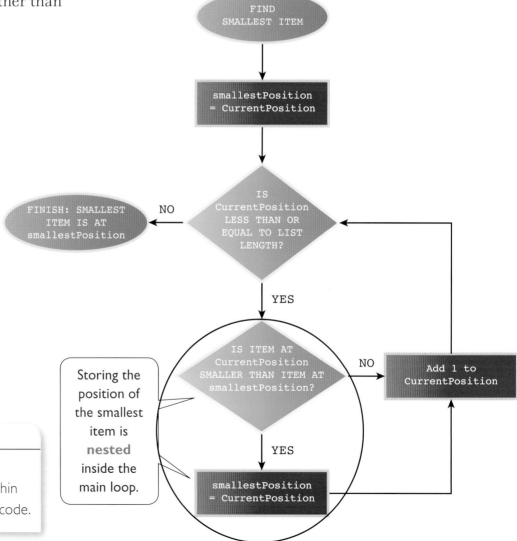

Storing the position of the smallest item is **nested** inside the main loop.

Key Term

Nesting: Placing a section of code within another section of code.

If **j** represents the position of the smallest item in the list, we need to find the value of **j**. To do this we must:

- create a variable called **smallestPosition** and set it to 1 to represent the first item in the list
- compare the value of the first item with the value of the next item in the list.

If the value of the next item in the list is smaller than the value of first item, the variable **smallestPosition** is updated to 2. If the value of the next item in the list is not smaller than the value of the first item, the variable **smallestPosition** is not updated. It stays as 1.

The value of the next item in the list is compared with the value that is currently in the **smallestPosition**. If the value of the next item is smaller, then the **smallestPosition** is updated with the position of the new smallest item and so on.

```
smallestPosition=1
FOR j=2 to List.Length
    IF list[j]<list[smallestPosition] THEN
        smallestPosition = j
    ENDIF
NEXT j
```

Now let's look at the algorithm as a whole, with the pseudocode for storing the position of the smallest item nested:

```
FOR i=1 TO List.Length
    smallestPosition=i
    FOR j=i TO List.Length
        IF List[j]<List[smallestPosition] THEN
            smallestPosition=j
        ENDIF
    NEXT j
    temp=List[i]
    List[i]=List[smallestPosition]
    List[smallestPosition]=temp
NEXT i
```

Compute-IT

7.5.1 Program Selection Sort in a graphical programming language, using the pseudocode to help you.

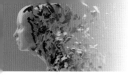
7.6 Comparing sorting algorithms

Which sorting algorithm is best?

The challenge for this unit is to write a program for a high-score table for a computer game, and you will need to create a sorting algorithm to do this. We have examined three sorting algorithms: BogoSort, Bubble Sort and Selection Sort. But which one should you use to complete the challenge? You need to compare them before you make your decision.

Deciding which algorithm is 'best' isn't a straightforward task. Some algorithms, like BogoSort, just aren't very good; some will perform well on certain sets of data but not so well on others and there are also lots of different criteria we could use for comparison. For example, you could consider how much memory a sorting algorithm requires. However, no one likes to wait longer than is absolutely necessary, so speed is critical when choosing a sorting algorithm for a real-world application and we are therefore going to use speed as our criterion for comparison. Once we have established our criterion we can then perform **empirical testing** to determine which algorithm ranks best against that criterion.

Empirically testing sorting algorithms

The experiment we design to test our sorting algorithms needs to consider:

- The quantity of data we will eventually use the best algorithm to sort, so that the experiment produces useful results. One algorithm might be considered to be the best if only a small quantity of data is being sorted, but might be ranked much lower in the list if a larger quantity of data is being sorted.
- The random nature of the data we will eventually use the best algorithm to sort, because we have already established that some algorithms are quicker at sorting data in a random order than others.
- If the data we will be expecting the sorting algorithm to sort is random, then it would be good

Think-IT

7.6.1 a) Rank BogoSort, Selection Sort and Bubble Sort in order, with the one you think is the best at the top and the one you think is the worst at the bottom.

b) What criteria did you use for deciding which was the best algorithm?

Key Term

Empirical testing: This is the name given to the process of testing something through experiment.

to test each sorting algorithm against more than one random data set and work out the average speed for each algorithm, just in case the random order chosen for one file favours one algorithm over another.

Compute-IT

7.6.2 **a)** Create the following nine lists:

- Five items in a random order
- Six items in a random order
- Seven items in a random order
- Nineteen items in reverse order
- Nineteen items with just one item out of order at the end of the list
- Nineteen items with just one item out of order at the beginning of the list
- Nineteen items in random order A
- Nineteen items in random order B
- Nineteen items in random order C

b) Time how long it takes Bubble Sort and Selection Sort to sort each list and record your findings in a table.

c) How much of an effect does the number of items have on each algorithm?

d) Which algorithm would you choose to sort data that is almost in order?

e) Which algorithm would you choose to sort randomly ordered data?

f) Which algorithm would be the best to program the high-score table for the computer game and why?

Challenge

Your challenge for this unit is to write a program for a high-score table for a computer game.

Compute-IT

7.6.3 Using what you have learned about sorting algorithms, write a program in a graphical programming language to store and sort high scores for a computer game.

You will need to create a list of high scores, something like this, which will need to be sorted:

108 Tereza	700 Chao	823 Betsy	283 Winnie
950 Joshua	680 Natalie	400 Lucinda	130 Amina
320 Hamish	381 Amit		

When a new game has been completed the new score should be added, the list should be sorted and the bottom score removed so there are only ever ten scores on the table.

Challenge

Your challenge is to make a computer appear intelligent by holding a conversation with a human.

8.1 Can computers think?

What is intelligence?

If we are to try to make a computer look intelligent, we first need to understand what intelligence is. This is not an easy thing to do. People have been debating intelligence for years and many now consider there to be different kinds of intelligence. For example, it is suggested that there is a difference between logical/mathematical intelligence and interpersonal or emotional intelligence.

In the context of computer science we need to ask ourselves, what exactly do we want a machine that appears to be intelligent to do?

We want an 'intelligent' machine to be able to figure things out. We want it to be able to:

- reason
- plan
- solve problems
- think abstractly
- understand complex ideas
- learn quickly
- learn from experience.

Think-IT

8.1.1 What have you done today that shows intelligence? Explain your answers.

Think-IT

8.1.2 a) Look at the list of tasks below. Rank them in order, with the task that you think requires most intelligence at the top and the task that requires least intelligence at the bottom. There is no correct order, so explain your thinking behind your ranking.

- Reading a map
- Reading a map upside down
- Solving a fiendish Sudoku puzzle
- Winning at chess
- Learning a poem
- Adding up your supermarket bill in your head

- Working out your score at darts by subtraction
- Playing a musical instrument in a concert
- Sensing that a friend is upset and finding the right words to comfort them
- Scoring a goal in a competitive football match

b) Compare your list with your partner. Have you ranked the items in the list differently? Why?

Keep it simple

One thing that intelligent computer scientists do is to look at a complicated situation and simplify it. They use the skills of decomposition, abstraction and generalisation to solve problems. This helps them see what is important and what is less important and not waste time or get into a mess looking at things that aren't relevant to the problem they are solving.

Rube Goldberg was an American cartoonist and inventor who dreamed up crazily complicated ways to solve problems. This example shows a self-operating napkin which makes use of levers, a parrot, a cigar lighter and a skyrocket in order to wipe the mouth after taking a spoonful of soup. ▶

Think-IT

8.1.3   Are there any rules in your school that are too complicated and could usefully be simplified?

Thinking

One of the things that is implied by intelligence is the ability to think. But what does 'thinking' mean? There is probably just as little agreement on what thinking is as there is about what intelligence is.

Thinking is a process that humans use to help them understand the physical, mental, emotional and spiritual worlds they live in. It allows us to, among many other things, judge, consider, imagine, reflect upon, form an opinion and make decisions. It allows us to carry out actions virtually, thinking them through rather than acting them out.

Think-IT

8.1.4   How many ways can you 'think' of to describe what 'thinking' is?

We are trying to make a computer look smart. Does a machine need to be able to think to be smart? Can a machine actually think? Many people have attempted to answer this last question because sometimes it seems that computers behave in such a clever way that they do what we think of as 'thinking'. However, the Dutch computer scientist Edsger Dijkstra said:

> The question of whether Machines Can Think ... is about as relevant as the question of whether Submarines Can Swim.

So perhaps asking if a machine is intelligent or can think is a waste of time. Perhaps we should concentrate on making them useful.

Think-IT

8.1.5   Is it helpful to wonder whether machines can be intelligent? Does it help us to create better computers?

◀ Edsger W. Dijkstra (1930–2002) was an influential computer scientist and winner of the 1972 Turing Award. He devised the algorithm that bears his name and which is still used for many things, including finding the shortest path between routers in a network. He also made perceptive and amusing comments about many aspects of computer science.

Think-IT

8.1.6 Find an online noughts and crosses program and try playing against the computer. What strategies do you use against the computer?

Think-IT

8.1.7 **a)** Playing chess requires a lot of thought. Players must form mental abstractions of the game so they can plan future moves. Successful chess players are often considered to be highly intelligent. However, it has long been possible to write computer programs that can defeat the best human chess players. Do you think this is evidence that computers can be intelligent?

b) Find an online chess program and try playing against the computer. Is it easy to defeat the computer?

c) Why do you think even the best chess players are often defeated by computer chess programs?

▲ A scene from War Games, a film from 1983 in which a student almost starts World War III after hacking into a military computer and only averts disaster by beating it at noughts and crosses.

Predicting the future

One computer application that most people are familiar with is predictive text. This is commonly used when typing text messages or in many other every day applications.

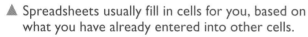

	A	B
1	**Forename**	**Surname**
2	Tyler	Rodriguez
3	Charlotte	Thompson
4	Lacey	Garcia
5	Angela	Mullins
6	Ivy	Conley
7	Adrienne	Bolton
8	Charlotte	

▲ Spreadsheets usually fill in cells for you, based on what you have already entered into other cells.

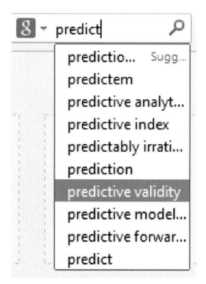

▲ Web browsers predict what you might want when entering search terms or URLs.

Humans perform the equivalent of predictive text all the time. If someone you know well is talking to you, it is often easy to figure out what they are going to say next because you have had similar conversations in the past. Computers also use information you have given them in the past to predict what you are going to want to do or say in the future. Computers don't always get it right though, do they? But, to be fair, do you?

Think-IT

8.1.8 What other common computer applications make predictions? What past data do they use?

Ultimately, it is difficult, if not pointless, to try to work out whether or not a machine is intelligent, whether what looks like intelligence actually is intelligence. It is more important that we develop machines that help us and that imitate intelligence to do this.

Think-IT

8.1.9   There are lots of machines on the market today that demonstrate some aspects of intelligence. Look at the photographs and decide to what extent each machine can:

- reason
- plan
- solve problems
- think abstractly

- understand complex ideas
- learn quickly
- learn from experience.

a)

b)

c)

d)

e)

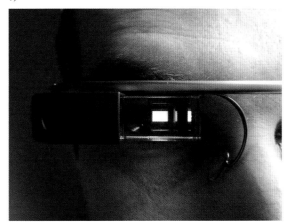

f)

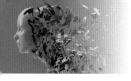

8.2 Input and output

Input, process, output

The purpose of nearly every computer program ever developed is to take in something from the real world, do something to it and then return a response of some sort. This input, process, output sequence can be seen in most applications. Here are just a few examples:

Application	INPUT	PROCESS	OUTPUT

SatNav	Signals from satellites
	Map data
	User requests
		Calculate:
		  position
		  speed
		  arrival time
			Display position on a map

Car engine management system	Signals from sensors such as fuel rate flow meter	Check against pre-set values	Send error message and signals to actuators such as cruise control mechanisms
QR code reader on phone	QR code	Convert code to number Look up product or service	Display information about the product or service

Washing machine control program	Inputs from:
	  temperature sensor
	  water level sensor
		Check against target values	Send signal to:
			  heater
			  motor

All programming languages allow input and output. Usually, the input is taken from an input device and stored as a **variable** or a collection of variables.

Intelligent output

A computer will only look smart if it responds to information that it is given in a natural and meaningful way.

A simple program that asks you for your name and then greets you by that name should look something like this when it is run:

> **Key Term**
>
> **Variable**: A named location in memory used to store data.

We need to get the computer to:

- ask for a name
- accept the response
- store the response in a variable
- make a suitable reply, using the name that is now stored in the variable.

This is our algorithm for the program, shown as a series of statements. We can also show the algorithm as a flowchart:

ASK FOR NAME

STORE NAME

OUTPUT MESSAGE AND NAME

Compute-IT

8.2.1 Using a text-based programming language, write a program to implement the algorithm above that asks you your name and then greets you by that name.

Think-IT

8.2.2 a) It is easy to get a computer to call us by our name, but does that make it look intelligent?

b) If you were having a conversation with a computer, what would it have to do to look intelligent?

In most conversations, responses vary according to what is said. A standard reply, that is output whatever was input, is not very smart, but it is possible to program a computer to make a decision and to choose which response to output based on the input.

The program will ask for a name and then ask the person for his or her age. It will respond with one message if the person is old enough to vote and a different message if they are not old enough to vote.

Here are two test runs of the program:

> The program will use the following basic relational operators:
> < or 'less than'
> > or 'greater than'
> <= or 'less than or equal to'
> >= or 'greater than or equal to'
> So >= 18 or 'greater than or equal to 18' is old enough to vote and <18 or 'less than 18' is not old enough to vote.

What is your name? Dotty

How old are you? 2

You are too young to vote, Dotty

>>>

What is your name? Cleopatra

How old are you? 18

Come on in and vote, Cleopatra

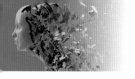
The age-checking algorithm looks like this:

Ask for name

Store name

Ask for age

Check that the person is over 18

If yes output success message

Else output fail message

Plan-IT

8.2.3 Draw a flowchart to plan the age-checking algorithm.

Compute-IT

8.2.4 Using a text-based programming language, write a program to implement the age-checking algorithm.

Key Term

Bug: An error in a computer program. This could be a flaw, failure or fault that produces incorrect or unexpected behaviour or results.

Testing

It is important that you test a program as thoroughly as you can, to convince yourself that it does what you planned. However, it can be difficult to think of all the possible inputs to a program, all the possible outputs it can produce and all the different pathways through the program. So, it is normal for programs to have errors or **bugs**, even after testing. A bug may only become apparent when a program is being used. In which case, the program has to be rewritten and retested to remove the bug.

Testing is used to show that a computer program does what it is intended to do when it receives expected inputs. But this is not all that testing does. A program that does exactly what it is supposed to do given expected inputs may behave in unexpected ways if it receives 'bad' inputs. So, testing is used to try to 'break' the program to reveal errors. A good test is a test that is likely to reveal an error. As a programmer you will often get attached to your work and will not always be motivated to try to break your programs or you may not always see the ways in which they could be broken. It is therefore a good idea for other programmers to test your programs.

During testing, you should consider:

- normal data, which is typical of what might be expected if the program was used normally
- extreme data, which is at the limits of what should be accepted or rejected
- abnormal data, which is not typical of what should be expected and should be rejected.

Here is another wise quote from Dijkstra on the subject of testing:

> Program testing can be used to show the presence of bugs, but never to show their absence!

Plan-IT

8.2.5 What tests do you think you need to carry out on the program you created for 8.2.4 Compute-IT? Explain why you think each test should be carried out.

Compute-IT

8.2.6 Carry out the tests that you listed in 8.2.5 Plan-IT. Record the test data entered, what you expect to happen, and what actually happens.

Multiple responses

We can make a conversation with a computer more interesting, and more 'intelligent', if we program the computer with multiple responses.

Think about phoning a bank. You might receive a menu of choices when you make the call. For example:

> Your call is valuable to us. So that we can best help you, please choose from the following options:
>
> Press 1 for your current balance
>
> Press 2 for your credit limit
>
> Press 3 to speak to an adviser
>
> Press 4 to give up

Plan-IT

8.2.7 Devise an algorithm for a simple menu system like the one shown above.

Compute-IT

8.2.8 Using a text-based programming language, write a program to implement the algorithm you devised for 8.2.7 Plan-IT.

Think-IT

8.2.9 What improvements could you make to the simple menu system to make it more useable?

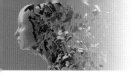
8.3 Developing a program

Iteration

Usually a conversation consists of more than one question and one answer. We can easily write a program that asks more than one question by using iteration and repeating parts of the program as many times as we need to.

A **loop** is a statement that allows a section of code to be executed a number of times. A loop can be used to add iteration to a program. There are several different types of loop, including 'for' loops, 'repeat until' loops and 'while … end while' loops.

'for' loops

A 'for' loop is used if it is known in advance how many times a loop needs to repeat. For example, if a program needs to ask a customer to input three numbers from their security code, the loop will need to repeat three times to assign the numbers to variables the program can use.

> **Key Term**
>
> **Loop**: Also known as a repeat, a loop is a statement that allows a section of code to be executed a number of times.

Your Security Number

Enter the following numbers from your Security Number

Enter the 4th number

Enter the 1st number

Enter the 3rd number

Entering a security number ▶

'repeat until' loops

Sometimes a program needs to keep repeating a section of code until something happens. This is normally controlled by a Boolean expression. As you know from Unit 5, **Boolean logic** is a form of algebra where all the answers can be reduced to True or False and stored in a Boolean variable. A **Boolean variable** can only ever have two values, 'true' or 'false'. No other result can be produced. For example:

> **Key Terms**
>
> **Boolean logic**: A form of algebra where all the answers can be reduced to true or false.
>
> **Boolean variable**: A variable that holds the value 'true' or 'false'.

$x=2$	Either **x** does equal 2 or it doesn't.
name='Fred'	Either the variable **name** contains the name 'Fred' or it doesn't.
$x>4$	Either **x** is greater than 4 or it isn't.

A 'repeat until' loop goes on repeating itself until a Boolean expression indicates a condition for it to end, a so-called **terminating condition**. This is why this type of loop is called a condition-controlled loop. The terminating condition is tested for at the end of the loop, so the loop must be entered at least once. So we might have a loop like this:

```
repeat
  print 'Enter name of item'
  input item
  print 'Another item?'
  input response
until response = 'n' or 'N'
```

'while ... end while' loops

'while ... end while' loops are also condition-controlled loops, but they differ from 'repeat until' loops in one way. They test for the condition *before* the loop starts rather than at the end. So, in some cases, the loop won't even be used.

Consider adding up a supermarket bill as items are scanned. As long as there's another item, the price is scanned and added to the bill and the program continues to loop. But, as soon as there are no more items to scan the loop is no longer required and it is not used again.

```
while item_scanned!=0
  total_bill=total_bill+item_cost
end while
```

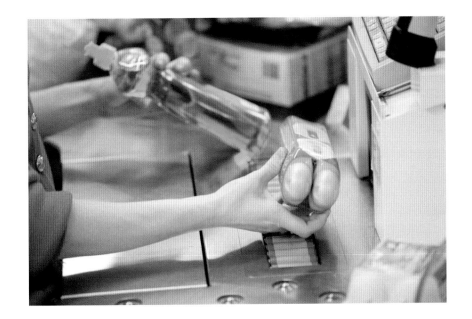

Key Term

Terminating condition: A condition used to test whether or not a loop should continue.

Plan-IT

8.3.1   Create an algorithm to show how a 'repeat until' loop can be used to make the menu program you created for 8.2.8 Compute-IT repeat itself until 'Give up' is chosen. Your algorithm can be a series of statements or a flowchart.

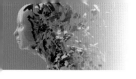
A 'repeat until' loop is a **post-tested loop**, because the condition is tested for at the end of the loop, so the loop must be entered at least once. A 'while end while' loop is a **top-tested loop** because the condition is tested before entering the loop and the loop may not be executed as a result.

Key Terms

Post-tested loop: The condition is tested for at the end of the loop, so the loop must be executed at least once.

Top-tested loop: The condition is tested before entering the loop and the loop may not be executed as a result.

Health warning

Loops are written in different ways in different languages. The main thing to remember is that some loops iterate a fixed number of times and others iterate as long as a condition is true and, in the case of a post-tested loop, will always loop at least once.

Sub-programs

The programmers who maintain program code are often not the same ones that wrote the original program, so it is important that programs are written in a clear and easily understandable way.

There are various ways to make sure that program code is easy to understand. For example, it is sensible to name variables in a way that indicates what they are for; it is better to use the variable name 'dob' for date of birth than something arbitrary like 'x'. It is also important to break programs down into **sub-programs**.

When you plan to build a house, you don't list all the things you need to do as you think of them, in a disorganised way. You have a master plan. Only when your master plan is in place do you concentrate on the component parts: the foundations, the walls, the roof, getting planning permission and all the other smaller projects that are involved in building a house. When we set out to write a program, we should plan it in the same way. We need to determine the big idea and then work out each sub-program that builds up to the big idea. The way you implement the solution will then depend on the programming language you chose to use.

Let's look again at the bank menu program. We have already produced a program that makes a few simple decisions so that it can respond to choices the caller makes

---

Key Term

Sub-program: A sub-program is a self-contained part of a larger program. It can be called as often as needed from other parts of the program.

with very simple replies. We could improve the program by having the computer ask more questions so that it has more information to work with and the response to the caller is more helpful. For instance, it would be useful to know the identity of the person calling and to verify that the caller is not an imposter. These details are needed for most of the options provided to the caller so it makes sense to collect them and then go to whichever option the customer wants.

Packaging the security questions in a sub-program has a lot of advantages. It makes the code:

- easier to write
- easier to maintain
- easier to test
- shorter.

It also makes it possible to reuse the code in other programs in the future.

Using sub-programs can hide the detailed processes, simplifying the structure of the main body of the program by putting them inside a sub-program. This is called **procedural abstraction**.

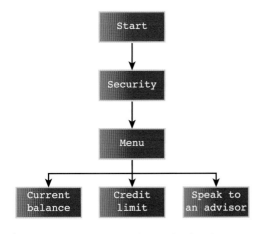

▲ A diagram showing how the bank menu program including security questions could be divided into sub-programs.

Key Term

Procedural abstraction: Combining a group of instructions into a single named unit so that it can be reused.

Plan-IT

8.3.3 Write an algorithm, as a series of statements or as a flowchart, to plan the new bank menu program containing a security sub-program. All you need do is to ask a set of security questions and repeat them back confirming the information. There is no need to look up customer details on a database. And the same security questions are asked regardless of whether it is Option 1, 2 or 3 that is selected.

Think-IT

8.3.2 What security questions and possible answers would a security sub-program for a telephone banking enquiry need to ask the caller?

Compute-IT

8.3.4 Using a text-based programming language, add a sub-program to the banking menu program you created for 8.2.8 Compute-IT, which is called by the main program when it is needed. Exactly how you program your sub-program will depend on the programming language you are using.

Think-IT

8.3.5 Does your program look intelligent yet? Explain your answer.

8.4 Storing responses

Data types

As you know, computers store data as a string of bits. These bits can represent anything we want them to including:

▲ Numbers

▲ Characters and words, which are groups of characters

▲ Music and other sounds

▲ Images

▲ Instructions. Program instructions themselves are stored as strings of bits

A computer program includes information about what sort of data the data being stored is. Each variable used in a program will be assigned a particular data type. Common examples of data types are:

- integer: the name given to the data type of whole numbers
- real: the name given to the data type of numbers with fractions
- character: the name given to the data type of letters and other symbols
- string: the name given to the data type of groups of characters
- Boolean: the name give to the data type of true or false values.

If a program is to make proper use of stored data, it needs to know what type each data item is so it can perform meaningful operations on it.

Programming languages have a wide variety of ways of storing data. In some languages, each variable has to be declared before it can be used. In other words, the programmer must make a decision at the outset about what data type is needed. This is called static typing. That means that once a data type is allocated to a variable, it stays like that for the whole program.

Here is an example of variable declaration in Visual Basic:

```
Dim num as Single
Dim name as String
```

The *Dim* statement sets up a variable, names it and allocates a data type to it. In this case, a variable called *num* is set up. It is allocated the data type of *Single*, which is a type of integer.

Some programming languages do not require variables to be declared or **initialised** before they can be used. They take their type dynamically when they are first used.

Key Term

Initialise: Set a variable to an initial value at the beginning of a program.

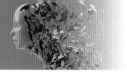

The variable *num* is given the value '4'. This makes *num* an integer.

The variable *name* is given the value 'Dotty'. It is a string because it is enclosed in quotes.

Here is a short piece of code written in Python Version 3.

```
num=4
real_num=5.6
name='Dotty'
print(num)
print(real_num)
print(name)
```

The variable *real_num* is given the value '5.6'. This makes *real_num* a real number with decimal places.

If you run this program you get the output you expect:

```
4
5.6
Dotty
```

But if you try to add **num** to **name** like this:

```
num=4
real_num=5.6
name='Dotty'
print(num)
print(real_num)
print(name)
result=num+name
print(result)
```

you get an error because the data types are mismatched. You can't add an integer to a string.

```
TypeError: unsupported operand type(s) for +:
'int' and 'str'
```

Think-IT

8.4.1 What data type will be useful for a program that is attempting to have a conversation with a human user?

Think-IT

8.4.2 List some of the problems you would encounter if you tried to set up lots of variables to store many similar values.

Storing multiple values

If we are trying to get a computer to have a simple conversation, it would be useful to store lots of words. We could do this by setting up lots of variables, like this:

```
Dim word1 as string
Dim word2 as string
```

But programming the words would quickly get tedious, and they would be very difficult to process.

Arrays and lists of elements

Most programming languages allow the programmer to use a **data structure** to hold a collection of items or elements. One of the simplest and most common data structures is an **array**. This is a finite **sequence** of **elements** that are all the same data type and that can be accessed by their position in the sequence. The number of possible elements in an array is fixed at the time the programmer creates the array.

> **Key Terms**
>
> **Data structure**: A data structure defines how to store and organise multiple items of data for convenient and efficient use of the data.
>
> **Array**: A data structure composed of a sequence of elements of the same type.
>
> **Sequence**: An ordered collection or list of one or more elements. Elements have a position in a sequence.
>
> **Element**: A single component of a data structure.

A simple array called **names**, holding a series of names, could look like this:

Data	Dotty	Bruno	Gary	Tristan	Isolde	Sieglinde	Cosima	Alma	Gustav
Index	0	1	2	3	4	5	6	7	8

You can put data into an array or get data out of one by referring to the name of the array and the **index** of the element you want. So, **names(3)** is 'Tristan'.

A list is a common data structure that is similar to an array. A list is a sequence of elements and can be used like an array. In addition, elements can usually be added to a list and the number of elements in the list can grow as needed. A list also allows the programmer easily to insert an element at an arbitrary position in the list and remove an element at an arbitrary position and the list is adjusted as needed.

> **Key Term**
>
> **Index**: The reference number that is used to refer to a single element in an array. It can also be called the 'subscript'.

Plan-IT

8.4.3 Find out how to program an array or list in your chosen text-based programming language. Be careful to get the **syntax** just right or it won't work.

Many programming languages support additional data structures that allow the programmer to organise and group data in different ways suited to a particular purpose. For example, there are data structures, such as tuples, that can be used to group multiple related items of different data types such as the name, age and gender of a person. You can, in other words, mix integers, real numbers and strings as much as you like. There are also data structures, called dictionaries, that are like lists except that they store data in pairs and they can be used to associate a key with a value just like a dictionary associates a word (the key) with its definition (the value).

Key Term

Syntax: The rules of a language. This definition applies to human languages as well as computer languages.

Plan-IT

8.4.4 Write an algorithm, as a series of statements or as a flowchart, to plan a program which does the following:

```
What is your name? Omar
Choose the number that shows your birth
  date:
1 March 21 — April 19
2 April 20 — May 20
3 May 21 — June 20
4 June 21 — July 22
5 July 23 — August 22
6 August 23 — September 22
7 September 23 — October 22
8 October 23 — November 21
9 November 22 — December 21
10 December 22 — January 19
11 January 20 — February 18
12 February 19 — March 20
What is your birth date? 3
Hello Omar
Your star sign is Gemini
```

Compute-IT

8.4.5 Write the program you planned in 8.4.4 Plan-IT using the information you collected in 8.4.3 Plan-IT to help you.

Compute-IT

8.4.6 Amend the horoscope program you created for 8.4.5 Compute-IT so that it provides predictions.

HINT: You could do this by making a second array or list with the predictions for each star sign in the same position in the index as the star signs in the star sign array or list. So, for example, you could have **star_sign(1)** being 'Aries' and **prediction(1)** being 'Today you will meet a mysterious stranger.'

◄ Zodiac with star sign symbols.

8.5 Randomness

Pseudo-random numbers

A conversation with a computer is more interesting if the responses the computer gives are less predictable. To achieve this we can introduce an element of randomness into the replies.

Random numbers are those taken from a set of numbers in such a way that each number has a genuinely equal chance of being selected. We learnt in *Compute-IT 1* that true randomness is difficult to achieve, because the factors that make for unpredictability can often, with enough information, be known and understood. In practice however, this doesn't matter much because we can program computers to produce numbers that appear to be random. These are called pseudo-random numbers and are good enough for most purposes.

One simple use of a random function is to produce a playlist for an MP3 player, where a chosen number of songs are played in an unpredictable order. If we take a list of 15 songs and store them in an array or a similar data structure we can program the computer to output however many songs we choose in a random order. We would end up with a list like this:

1 `All these things that I've done`

2 `Little talks`

3 `In the end`

4 `Give me love`

5 `In the end`

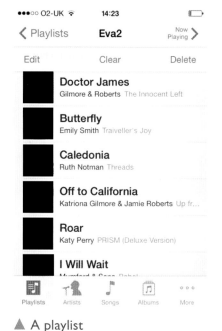

▲ A playlist

Plan-IT

8.5.1   Find out how to produce pseudo-random numbers in your chosen text-based programming language.

Plan-IT

8.5.2   Write an algorithm, as a series of statements or a flowchart, for a short program for an MP3 player that can randomly select five songs from a list of at least 15.

Compute-IT

8.5.3 Using your chosen text-based programming language, write the program you planned for 8.5.2 Plan-IT.

Compute-IT

8.5.4 Develop the program you wrote for 8.5.3 Compute-IT so that the user can choose how many songs are randomly selected from the stored list to produce the random playlist. Remember to test the program as you work, to make sure that the correct number of songs is always extracted.

Think-IT

8.5.6 Imagine you need some help to come up with ideas for a birthday present for a friend. You have decided to develop a computer program that stores any number of possible ideas and then matches them to the friend's preferences and will include a random function so the suggested ideas are more varied and interesting. You will start with small data sets to keep things relatively simple, but could expand the data sets later so the program has more possible ideas to choose from and can provide more sophisticated advice.

Think of a few questions you could ask your friend to establish their present preferences, and then ask someone to answer the questions.

Think-IT

8.5.5 You will have noticed that the program you have written allows songs to be repeated. What could you do to change the program to make sure this doesn't happen and each song only appears once in any one random playlist?

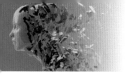

Plan-IT

8.5.7 Write an algorithm for a program, which includes sub-programs, that will:

- ask the name of your friend
- ask a few questions about your friend's interests
- store a few examples of presents in different categories
- match the interests to a randomly chosen present in the correct category.

Make decisions about how the program will be constructed to store the data logically and to separate the different functional parts of the program. Your algorithm can be presented as a series of statements or a flowchart.

Compute-IT

8.5.8 Using your chosen text-based programming language, write the program you planned for 8.5.7 Plan-IT.

A typical session with the completed program should look something like this:

What is your friend's name? Fred

Which of these interests your friend Fred?

Choose one from the list.

1 Sport

2 Reading

3 Fashion

4 Music

5 None of the above

Make your selection: 2

The ideal present for Fred is a Hodder Education textbook

Compute-IT

8.5.9 a) Write a list of tests that you could perform to check that the program you wrote for 8.5.8 Compute-IT is performing as intended.

b) Carry out the tests and write down what happened.

Think-IT

8.5.10 Are the tests that you carried out for 8.5.9 Compute-IT adequate for you to say that the program performs perfectly?

Compute-IT

8.5.11 Ask someone else to test your program by actively looking for faults. Can they make your program crash? Write a detailed report of what they did and what happened.

8.6 Is a computer really smart?

Can humans talk to computers?

Throughout this unit so far we have explored several ways to get a simple computer program to have some sort of conversation with a human. A lot of programs do this at a basic level and they provide us with all sorts of services. Booking a theatre ticket online is one situation where we interact with a computer system and arrive at a desired result.

Select Seats

BRB - Beauty and the Beast
Birmingham Hippodrome
Tuesday, 30 September, 2014 - 7:30pm Change Date
Good availability

VIEW SEATING PLAN   360 VIEWER

Do you have a promotion code?
Enter a code here to see special offers:

In order to purchase a Half Price Child discount you must first select a Full Price seat. Please note that two children may go half price with every full paying adult.

SELECT YOUR OWN SEAT   **SELECT BEST AVAILABLE**

Please click on your selected seat(s) and choose the relevant price(s). You must click "Add to Basket" at the bottom of the page. A maximum of 9 seats can be selected per booking. **Where possible, please do not leave single seats.**   OCCUPIED   AVAILABLE   + INFO   SAME PRICE   SELECTED

CHOOSE SECTION   **CHOOSE SEATS**   **PHOTO PREVIEWS**

CIRCLE
Row D Seat 9

Standard	£37.00	SELECT
Child	£34.00	SELECT
Student	£34.00	SELECT
Jobseeker	£34.00	SELECT
Over 60	£34.00	SELECT
Disabled/no W-Chair	£32.00	SELECT
Passport to Leisure	£34.00	SELECT
VIP Experience	£95.50	SELECT
StageSide Experienc	£79.00	SELECT

NAVIGATE MAP

ZOOM

Direction of Stage

Seats are not reserved until added to the shopping basket   No Seats Yet Selected   **ADD TO BASKET**

If you need help with your online transaction, or have any disabled access requirements please call **0844 338 5050** or email

When booking a theatre ticket online we have a conversation with the booking system where we:

- choose a part of the theatre
- see what seats are available
- choose our seats
- pay for our tickets
- collect our tickets.

Think-IT

8.6.1 Could a user be fooled into thinking that an interaction like purchasing a theatre ticket online was with a human being rather than a computer? What are the clues that give away that this is a human–computer interaction?

Think-IT

8.6.2 Here is another interaction or conversation:

```
* Hello Eliza, nice to meet you.
> Oh...   ?
* You are surprised?
> What makes you think I am surprised?
* Your exclamation of "Oh..."
> Why are you concerned about my exclamation of" Oh..."?
* Because you are clearly not used to being greeted
pleasantly.
> Do you sometimes wish you were clearly not used to
being greeted pleasantly?
* All the time. I hate it.
> What does that suggest to you?
```

Input: [   ]

Does this look a bit like a typical IM session? What makes it look like an online conversation and what does not? How easy is it to tell who is the human and who is the computer?

The conversation shown in 8.6.2 Think-IT is an output from one of the oldest attempts to create a program that allows a computer to have a 'conversation' with a human. The program is called Eliza and it first appeared in the 1960s. There are now many versions of Eliza on the internet. Eliza is programmed to take something from what the human says and feed it back with some randomised comment. This makes it look a little as if Eliza is listening and reacting appropriately to the human inputs. Eliza was devised to be a spoof computerised psychotherapist so if some of the replies turn out to be gobbledegook, it is not necessarily surprising!

Think-IT

8.6.3 Search for 'Eliza' on the internet and have a conversation with her.

The Turing Test

Alan Turing was, as you know from *Compute-IT 1*, one of the most important figures in the development of computers. He set the scene for them by describing how a machine – as yet not invented – could produce a wide variety of computed results depending on the instructions given to it. The Turing Machine was entirely hypothetical but it led, in a very short time, to the production of real computers that could indeed be programmed to produce a wide range of computed results.

▲ Alan Turing, 1912–1954

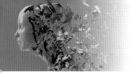
Turing was also interested in the possibility of artificial intelligence, which was a big leap forward at a time when real computers still did not exist. He devised a simple way of determining if a machine was intelligent, a method known as the Turing Test. This is still widely accepted as a possible benchmark for assessing artificial intelligence. The test is designed to tell if a machine can be made to behave in the same way as a human.

In the Turing Test, you imagine a conversation between a human and a machine and another human. The human cannot see the machine and the other human and communicates only by text. This prevents signals such as tone of voice or body language from giving the game away. If the human doing the test cannot tell which answers are from the machine and which are from the human, the machine is deemed to be 'intelligent'.

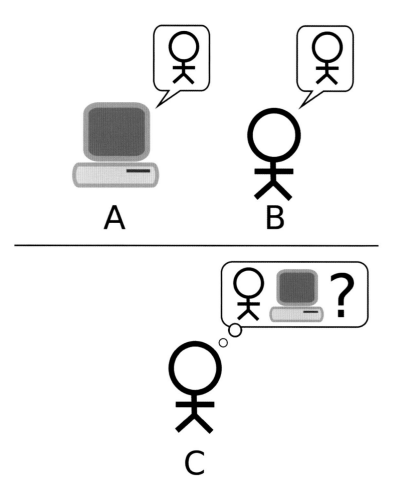

Think-IT

8.6.4 Do you think Eliza would pass the Turing Test? Explain your answer.

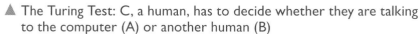
▲ The Turing Test: C, a human, has to decide whether they are talking to the computer (A) or another human (B)

Challenge

Do you remember the challenge for this unit, to make a computer appear intelligent by holding a conversation with a human?

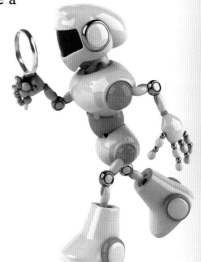

We have written several programs so far that give feedback and it could be argued that they are holding 'conversations' with the user in a very limited way. Introducing random functions makes these programs appear a little more 'human' because, in a real conversation with a human, you can't normally predict exactly what the other person will say. However, we do have a way to go before our programs appear 'intelligent', and we can take a few clues from Eliza.

Features of a conversation

For a computer to have a convincing conversation with a human it should:

- answer in a relevant way
- show that it has been listening to the human
- sometimes be surprising
- sometimes change the subject.

Features of our program

This means our program should:

- have a store of answers
- connect the human statements to a (fairly) relevant answer
- allow for unrecognisable inputs
- use some, but not too much, randomness in order to simulate unexpected human responses.

Writing a conversation program

When writing a conversational program, it is probably best to limit the conversation to a single topic. That way, we can keep the bank of responses down to a manageable level, although at the cost of being less realistic. So let's simulate a doctor–patient consultation.

First, we store some symptoms and responses to them. For example, if the patient says, 'I have a pain', the doctor can reply, 'It will probably go away'. Or, if the doctor is any good, he or she will ask more questions.

We have a problem here, though. When we were looking at choosing birthday presents, we set up the program so that the user picked from a list. We did this so that the input was restricted to a few allowable answers. This reduced the chance of the human saying something that the computer didn't understand.

But this would not seem natural for a doctor–patient consultation. Imagine going to the doctor and selecting from a fixed list of symptoms! Ideally, we want a conversation to be in **natural language**. Getting a computer to understand natural language is not easy. Getting it to reply in natural language is harder still.

The human patient will want to talk in natural language. One way we can get the computer to understand is to search what the patient says for key words. So, if the patient says, 'I have a pain', the algorithm scans the statement for key words – in this case, 'pain' – and constructs a response based on those key facts.

So, at a simple level, we can store some symptoms and responses and search for the appropriate response based on key words contained within the symptoms. Here is a possible interaction:

Key Term

Natural language: Natural language is the way that humans speak. Natural language has developed informally, in contrast to formal programming languages that have strict rules of syntax and construction.

Doctor: Tell me what troubles you

Patient: I feel sick

Doctor: Stop eating bad food then

Just in case the patient says something unexpected, you need a backup plan:

Doctor: Tell me what troubles you

Patient: I have a spot on my nose

Doctor: I don't know anything about that. Find another doctor

Plan-IT

8.6.5 Imagine a doctor–patient consultation where the doctor has very limited knowledge. Draw up an algorithm, as a series of statements or a flowchart, to deal with one symptom and one response in natural language.

Compute-IT

8.6.6 Using your chosen text-based programming language, write the program you planned for 8.6.5 Plan-IT.

HINT: The programming language you are using will probably have a function such as **in** that lets you easily scan input for a particular word or phrase.

We will now write a program that can continue having a conversation as long as the human wants to.

Plan-IT

8.6.7 Your program will need three places to store data. Invent suitable phrases to go in the first two:

- start-up questions
- follow-up questions and statements that can be used to keep the conversation going
- the human's responses when they are received. These are stored so that they can be used by the program in its reply to make it seem as if the computer is listening to the human.

Try to make the phrases work with a wide variety of human inputs.

Plan-IT

8.6.8 Draw up an algorithm, as a series of statements or a flowchart, that allows a computer to have a fairly natural conversation with a human, using the human's responses in its replies. The program also needs some use of randomness in order to make the responses a bit more natural, and it needs to loop continuously until the human user terminates the conversation by making no remark and then pressing enter.

Compute-IT

8.6.9 Using your chosen text-based programming language, write the program you planned for 8.6.8 Plan-IT.

Compute-IT

8.6.10 Test the program to ensure it works technically.

Think-IT

8.6.11 The program wouldn't fool many people and would certainly have a hard time passing the Turing Test. What aspects could be improved to make it a bit more convincing?

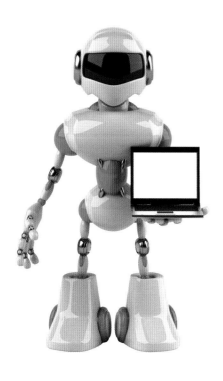

Challenge

You are going to become pattern detectives and investigate some of the ways in which patterns can be created in mathematics, art and music using computers. You will use your new-found knowledge of recursive patterns to write a program that enables a computer to output a recursive pattern.

9.1 Decomposing songs to find recursive patterns

Recursion

Patterns can be described in a number of ways. For example, they can be regular, radial or serial. They can also be recursive. A recursive pattern is a pattern where the pattern or part of the pattern is repeated inside a part of the pattern, which is repeated inside a part of the pattern. Recursive patterns are often referred to as self-referential, because they refer to themselves.

In computing, a recursive program is one that calls itself or a part of itself over and over again until it reaches a finishing point and returns to where the **recursion** began. Recursion is used in computing to cut down on the amount of code that has to be programmed, because a section of code can be repeated – iterated – again and again within the program.

Key Term

Recursion: In computing, a recursive program is one that calls itself or a part of itself over and over again until it reaches a finishing point and returns to where the recursion began.

Think-IT

9.1.1   As acronyms are very common in computing, computer programmers have used them on a number of occasions to smuggle recursion into the names of things. The acronyms 'PHP' and 'GNU' are both recursive. Why?

▲ This is a regular pattern. There is the same amount of space between each shape.

▲ This is a radial pattern. It is made up of straight lines that move out from the centre of a circle.

▲ This is a serial pattern. The shapes are arranged in a series or form part of a series.

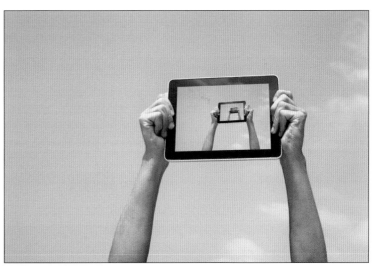

▲ This is a recursive pattern. The man looking into the tablet is inside the image of the man looking into the tablet.

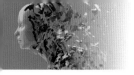

Recursion in *One Man Went to Mow*

We can see recursion in the song *One Man Went to Mow*:

One man went to mow, went to mow a meadow,
One man and his dog, Woof! Went to mow a meadow.

Two men went to mow, went to mow a meadow,
Two men, one man and his dog, Woof! Went to mow a meadow.

Three men went to mow, went to mow a meadow,
Three men, two men, one man and his dog, Woof! Went to mow a meadow.

Four men went to mow, went to mow a meadow,
Four men, three men, two men, one man and his dog, Woof! Went to mow a meadow.

Five men went to mow, went to mow a meadow,
Five men, four men, three men, two men, one man and his dog, Woof! Went to mow a meadow.

For each verse, one is added to the red value, the words highlighted in green are repeated and an extra bit of text is added to the beginning of the second line. So we could think of the song in the following way:

First verse
Verse number = 1
(Verse number) man went to mow, went to mow a meadow.
One man and his dog, Woof! Went to mow a meadow.

Second verse
Add 1 to the verse number
(Verse number) men went to mow, went to mow a meadow.
(Verse number) men (Verse 1)

And Verse 3
Add 1 to the verse number
(Verse number) men went to mow, went to mow a meadow.
(Verse number) men (Verse 2)
And so on...

Plan-IT

9.1.2 a) Create an algorithm to output 10 verses of *One Man Went to Mow*.

b) What would you need to change to output five verses of the song? What about 100 verses?

When writing a recursive program, it is not enough to write a program that just calls itself. If you do that you will end up with a program that runs forever and eventually crashes itself or the computer it is running on because it will use up all the available resources. A recursive program should, eventually, reach a point where the program stops calling itself. This point, the 'termination condition', is called the **base case**.

Key Term

Base case: The terminating condition for a recursive loop.

Plan-IT

9.1.3 Create an algorithm to output the song *Ten Green Bottles*. Think about what changes and what stays the same in each verse.

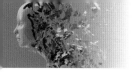

9.2 Writing recursive programs

Recursive sub-programs

A recursive program calls itself and has a way of terminating, a base case. But how do we code a recursive program?

Most iterative programs that contain loops can be altered to become recursive programs. We just call a specific part of the program – be it a sub-program, a function or a procedure – to create the recursive call.

We can define a recursive process that counts down from one to three, in Scratch 2.0 like this:

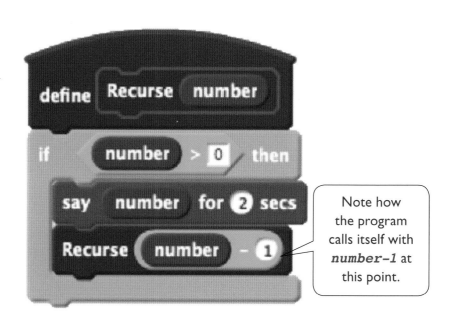

Note how the program calls itself with *number–1* at this point.

Compute-IT

9.2.1 Type in and then modify the recursive Python Version 3 program, so that it counts down from a number input by the user.

And in Python Version 3 like this:

```
# sub program
def recurse(number):
if number>0:
print(number)
recurse(number-1)
#main program
recurse(3)
```

Factorials

The symbol ! is used to signify the factorial of a number. The factorial of a number is all the whole numbers less than or equal to the number multiplied together so $3! = 3 \times 2 \times 1 = 6$ and $4! = 4 \times 3 \times 2 \times 1 = 24$. If you look carefully you will see that 4! can be written as $4 \times 3!$ It can be defined recursively.

Plan-IT

9.2.2 This algorithm shows how we can describe 2! recursively.

Copy this and extend it to show how we can define 5! recursively.

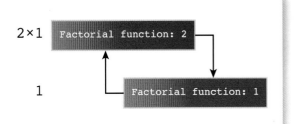

To avoid problems, mathematicians have defined 0! as 1, which allows us to write an algorithm for a sub-program to calculate a factorial for a number.

```
#sub program
define factorial(number)
  if number = 0 then return 1
  else
  return number*factorial(number-1)
```

Compute-IT

9.2.3 a) Using the algorithm you created for 9.2.2 Plan-IT to help you, write a recursive program to calculate 5! in a text-based programming language.

b) Modify your program to allow it to calculate a factorial for a number input by the user.

Compute-IT

9.2.5 Using the algorithm you created for 9.1.2a Plan-IT to help you, create a program in a graphical programming language that sings the song *One Man Went to Mow*.

Plan-IT

9.2.4 a) Identify the phrases you will need if you are going to write a program that sings *One Man Went to Mow*. You want your program to be efficient, so you should use the minimum number of phrases possible.

b) Create an audio file for each phrase you have identified and save the files in one folder with logical file names.

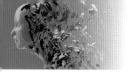
9.3 The Fibonacci Series and the Golden Ratio

The Fibonacci Series

One thousand three hundred years ago Leonardo of Pisa, or Fibonacci as he became known, described the following problem:

> How many pairs of rabbits will be produced at the end of one year from one pair of rabbits, if each pair produces a new pair each month, each new pair starts reproducing at the age of one month, and no rabbits die?

In solving the problem, the Fibonacci Series of numbers was established. It is a series of numbers formed by adding the two previous numbers together.

Number of pairs

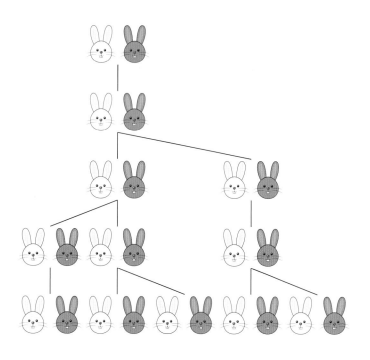

1

1   We start the series with 1, 1

2   The next value is 1 + 1 = 2

3   The next value is 1 + 2 = 3

5   And the next value is 2 + 3 = 5

Think-IT

9.3.1   What are the next five numbers in the Fibonacci Series?

An algorithm to print out the Fibonacci Series is:

```
set a and b to 1
set c to 2
print a
while c <= 10
    print b
    temp = a
    a = b
    b = b + temp
    c = c + 1
```

As we saw in Unit 7, we use a variable, called 'temp', to enable us to swap numbers.

Compute-IT

9.3.2 Create a program in a text-based programming language to print out the first 10 numbers of the Fibonacci Series.

The Golden Ratio

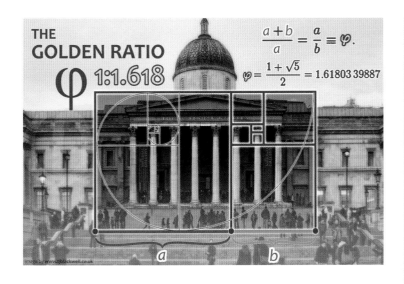

THE GOLDEN RATIO

φ 1:1.618

$$\frac{a+b}{a} = \frac{a}{b} \equiv \varphi.$$

$$\varphi = \frac{1 + \sqrt{5}}{2} = 1.61803\,39887$$

Think-IT

9.3.3 a) Using a spreadsheet, work out the first 20 numbers in the Fibonacci Series.

b) Still using your spreadsheet, take each number in the Fibonacci Series and divide it by the number in the Series that immediately precedes it. For example:

1	1	2	3	5
	1/1	2/1	3/2	5/3

c) Plot the results on a graph. What do you notice?

You should have discovered that the further you work through the Fibonacci Series the closer the calculation you perform homes in on a specific value. This value, 1.61803398875, is known to mathematicians as the Golden Ratio, or Phi (φ), and there is a populist belief that it describes the ratio between the sides of various rectangles.

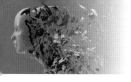
The Fibonacci Series and the Golden Ratio working together in nature

If we draw a one-unit square and place another square 1 unit by 1 unit next to it we get this:

If we add a two-unit square below the shape we have drawn, using one of the sides of our shape as one of the sides for the new square we end up with this:

If we continue adding larger and larger squares in an anticlockwise spiral, with each new square using the existing shape to govern the length of its side, we end up with a drawing like this:

If we draw the spiral made by the pattern we can see that it looks like a nautilus shell:

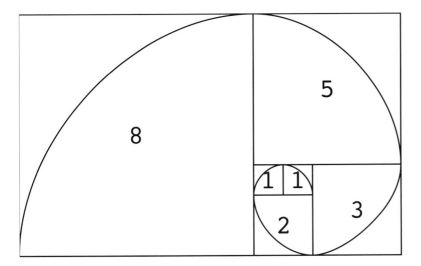

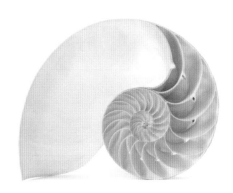

▲ Plants grow new cells in a spiral. They create a new cell then turn, create another cell and turn again, and so on. The amount turned is important because turning the wrong amount can leave a gap. The amount they turn is 0.618 – the Golden Ratio – which as we know creates a pattern with no gaps from start to end.

▲ When plants grow, the pattern of leaves at each level follows the Fibonacci Series.

Think-IT

9.3.4 Find images of three natural objects that illustrate the Golden Ratio at work and show how the Golden Ratio can be seen in each object.

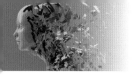

Compute-IT

9.3.5 a) The Lucas Series uses the same principles as the Fibonacci Series but changes the starting numbers to a '2' and a '1' so the series begins:

2, 1, 3

What are the first 20 numbers in the Lucas Series?

b) Compare the first 20 numbers in the Fibonacci Series with the first 20 numbers in the Lucas Series. Do the two sequences have any values in common?

Compute-IT

9.3.6 Modify the program you created for 9.3.2 Compute-IT so that you can input any two starting values and can choose how many numbers to print.

Compute-IT

9.3.7 Modify the program you created for 9.3.6 Compute-IT further so that it prints out the ratio of the numbers.

The Fibonacci Series is a recursive pattern, because it is defined in terms of its previous values. The algorithm for a sub-program to generate the Fibonacci Series recursively is:

```
define fib()
if n=0 then
  return 0
else if n=1 then
  return 1
else return fib(n-1) + fib(n-2)
```

Compute-IT

9.3.8 Using the algorithm provided, create a recursive program in a text-based programming language to output the Fibonacci Series. Include an option for the user to select how many numbers they want to output.

9.4 Outputting patterns from recursive programs

Challenge

Do you remember the challenge for this unit? It's time to write a recursive program that enables a computer to output one or more of the following recursive patterns:

- one of the times tables 1 to 12
- triangular numbers
- square numbers.

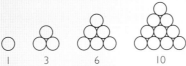

▲ Triangular numbers

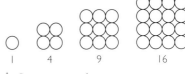

▲ Square numbers

In each case the user should be able to select the values to use to output or the number of terms for the sequence.

It is important we document programs fully when we write them so that they can be maintained in the future. We should explain our analysis of the problem and what we are trying to do. We also need to document our approach to the problem using algorithms to describe our solution. When we create the code we should test it to make sure it works under most conditions and we need to document this testing process so that others will know what has already been tested and how in case a problem occurs in the program. We also use meaningful variable names and add comments to our code to explain how it works and what different sections of code do. We put all this evidence together with our evaluation of the solution into project documentation.

Compute-IT

9.4.1 Decompose the problem and write a program in natural language.

9.4.2 Perform recursive thinking to create an algorithm for your recursive program.

9.4.3 Write your recursive program using a text-based programming language.

9.4.4 Test and debug your recursive program.

9.4.5 Comment on your recursive program.

9.4.6 Write a report explaining design, implementation and functionality of your program, and describing how you could extend it.

Glossary / Index

Acknowledgements

The Publishers would like to thank the following for permission to reproduce copyright material:

Photo credits:

All robot images used in Challenge boxes © julien tromeur – Fotolia.com.

All Scratch blocks © Scratch (http://scratch.mit.edu/), used with kind permission.

Header image © adimas–Fotolia

p. 3 *l* and *r* © Apple Inc.; **p. 4** Courtesy of Jonathan Zander (Digon3)/Wikipedia Creative Commons (http://commons.wikimedia.org/wiki/Commons:GNU_Free_Documentation_License_1.2); **p. 5** *l* Courtesy of Wikipedia Commons (http://en.wikipedia.org/wiki/File:Award_BIOS_setup_utility. png), *r* © creative soul – Fotolia.com; **p. 8** *l* Used with permission from Microsoft, *m* © Apple Inc., *r* Source Larry Ewing/Linux; **p. 9** *t* Used with permission from Microsoft., *b*© Apple Inc.; **p. 10** *l* Used with permission from Microsoft, *m* © Apple Inc., *r* © STANCA SANDA / Alamy; **p. 11** © Lisa F. Young – Fotolia.com; p. 13 © sima – Fotolia.com; **p. 14** Used with permission from Microsoft; **p. 16** Used with permission from Microsoft; **p. 17** © Apple Inc.; **p. 20** © Artur Marciniec – Fotolia.com; **p. 21** *b* © Stephen Dorey ABIPP / Alamy; *t* © Monty Rakusen / Cultura / Getty Images, **p. 24** © Edelweiss – Fotolia.com; **p. 29** *t* © mkos83 – Fotolia.com; *b* © INTERFOTO / Alamy; **p. 31** © Francesco Marciuliano; **p. 32** © Lightbot. Inc (http://light-bot.com); **p. 33** *t* MB Electronics Big Trak Courtesy of Tomhannen / Wikimedia Commons (http://en.wikipedia.org/wiki/GNU_Free_Documentation_License), *b* Courtesy NASA/JPL-Caltech; **p. 34** Screenshots supplied by Sharon McTeir; **p. 35** © finallast – Fotolia.com; **p. 36** © TTS Group (www.tts-group.co.uk); **p. 37** © Bubbles Photolibrary / Alamy; **p. 38** *l* © S_E – Fotolia. com, *r* © REX/Frederic Sierakowski; **p. 40** © AA+W – Fotolia.com; **p. 41** © FRANK RUMPENHORST/ AFP/Getty Images; **p. 44** Courtesy NASA/JPL-Caltech; **p. 45** Courtesy of Bill Bertram 2006, CC-BY-2.5 / Wikipedia Creative Commons (http://creativecommons.org/licenses/by-sa/2.5/deed.en); **p. 47** Courtesy Rurik / Wikipedia Creative Commons (http://en.wikipedia.org/wiki/File:Longleat_maze. jpg); **p. 52** © xy – Fotolia.com; **p. 53** Courtesy of Seasalt (www.seasaltcornwall.co.uk); **p. 55** © REX/ Snap Stills; **p. 57** © Focus Pocus LTD – Fotolia.com; **p. 64** © carloscastilla – Fotolia.com; **p. 65** © Skyscan Photolibrary / Alamy; **p. 72** © Steve Connolly; **p. 74** © YAY Media AS / Alamy; **p. 75** © Knoema (http:// knoema.com/atlas/maps/internet-users-per-100-inhabitants); **p. 76** © zentilia – Fotolia.com; **p. 77** *t* © mbongo – Fotolia.com, *b* © Olexandr – Fotolia.com; **p. 80** Courtesy of The Opte Project / Wikipedia Commons (http://creativecommons.org/licenses/by/2.5/deed.en); **p. 82** The London Underground logo is a registered trade mark of Transport for London; **p. 83** © Macmen – Fotolia.com; **p. 86** © David Gee 5 / Alamy; **p. 94** Courtesy of Seasalt (www.seasaltcornwall.co.uk); **p. 95** *tl* Courtesy Sharon McTeir, *bl* © iPhone / Alamy, *tr* © Touch – Fotolia.com; **p. 103** Monica Wanjie; **p. 109** Artwork Copyright © and TM Rube Goldberg Inc. All Rights Reserved. RUBE GOLDBERG ® is a registered trademark of Rube Goldberg Inc. All materials used with permission. rubegoldberg.com; **p. 111** *t* © Andreas F. Borchert / Wikipedia Commons (http://creativecommons.org/licenses/by-sa/3.0/de/deed.en), *b* © REX/Moviestore Collection; **p. 113** *tl* © Unclesam – Fotolia.com, *tr* © yevgeniy11 – Fotolia.com, *ml* © RTimages – Fotolia.com, *mr* © Dorling Kindersley – Getty Images *bl* © Rex, *br* © Internet Addiction / Moment Editorial/Getty Images; **p. 117** © Eugenio Marongiu – Fotolia.com; **p. 119** © PhotoAlto / Alamy; **p. 122** *tl* © pixel_dreams – Fotolia.com, *ml* © kacperogo – Fotolia.com, *tr* © strahlendeslicht – Fotolia.com, *bl* © DAN -Fotolia.com, *br* © jamdesign – Fotolia.com; **p. 127** © jvphoto / Alamy; **p. 128** Screenshot taken by Sharon McTeir; **p. 129** © Juice Images / Alamy; p. 130 *t* © karandaev – Fotolia.com, *b* © Andres Rodriguez – Fotolia.com; **p. 131** © Michael Soo / Alamy; **p. 132** Courtesy of Birmingham Hippodrome (www.birminghamhippodrome.com); **p. 133** © The Granger Collection / TopFoto; **p. 134** Courtesy of Bilby / Wikipedia Commons (http://en.wikipedia.org/wiki/File:Turing_Test_version_3. png); **p. 136** © Paul Hakimata – Fotolia.com; **p. 137** © REX/Nils Jorgensen; **p. 139** *tl* © creative_stock – Fotolia.com, *tr* © saga1966 – Fotolia.com, *bl* © boomingpie - Fotolia.com, *br* © anyaberkut – Fotolia. com; **p. 141** © Image Source / Alamy; **p. 145** © tj.blackwell – Flickr (https://www.flickr.com/photos/ tjblackwell/8313250246/); p. 147 *t* © barneyboogles – Fotolia.com, *bl* © Tanya Ru – Fotolia.com, *br* © Jill Britton (jbmathfun.com);

t = top, b = bottom, l = left, r = right, m = middle

Every effort has been made to trace all copyright holders, but if any have been inadvertently overlooked the Publishers will be pleased to make the necessary arrangements at the first opportunity.